A STUDY OF THE REVELATION

Esther Onstad

AUGSBURG PUBLISHING HOUSE
Minneapolis, Minnesota

COURAGE FOR TODAY HOPE FOR TOMORROW

Copyright © 1973, 1974 Augsburg Publishing House

First paperback edition, 1975

Library of Congress Catalog Card No. 75-2829

International Standard Book No. 0-8066-1474-9

Scripture quotations unless otherwise noted are from the Revised Standard Version of the Bible, copyright 1946, 1952, and 1971 by the Division of Christian Education of the National Council of Churches.

Manufactured in the United States of America

TABLE OF CONTENTS

COURAGE FOR TODAY—
HOPE FOR TOMORROW

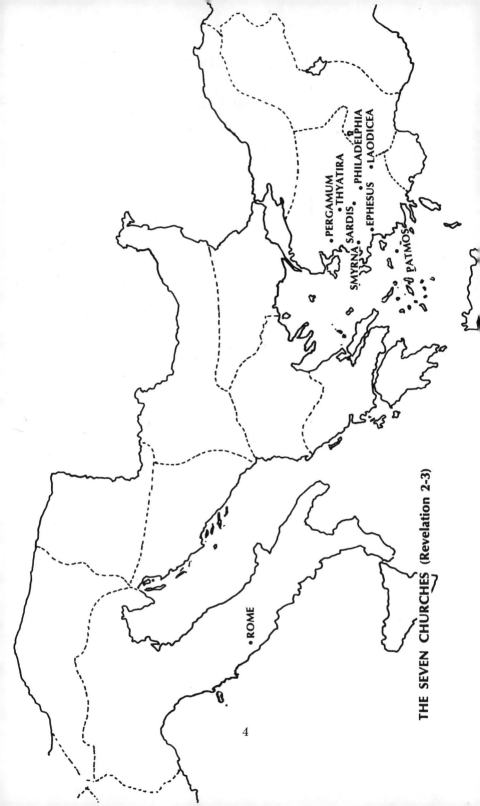

THE SEVEN CHURCHES (Revelation 2-3)

PERGAMUM
THYATIRA
SARDIS
SMYRNA
PHILADELPHIA
LAODICEA
EPHESUS
PATMOS

ROME

4

OUTLINE CHART OF THE REVELATION

CHAPTER TITLES	SUMMARY OF KEY IDEAS	
1. Christ Is Alive!	Christ is in the midst of his church, helping, encouraging, warning	**PREPARATION**
2. Messages to the & 3. Seven Churches		
4. God on the Throne	Christ is in control of history	
5. The Lamb and the Scroll		
6. THE SEALS	Beginning of Judgments	**CONFLICT: Invisible—Christ vs. Satan / Visible—Church vs. The World**
7. "Behold a Host!"	Christians are secure	
8. THE TRUMPET 9. JUDGMENTS	More severe judgments no repentance	
10. Angel and the Book	Preparation for final judgments. Underlying cause of conflict—the dragon, the beast out of the sea and the beast of the land.	
11. Two Witnesses		
12. Woman and the Child		
13. Two Beasts		
14. Songs on Mt. Zion	Persecuted and martyred church sings songs of triumph and victory	
15. Song of Moses and the Lamb		
16. BOWLS OF WRATH	Final judgment most severe Every enemy defeated. Christ proclaimed KING OF KINGS AND LORD OF LORDS	**VICTORY**
17. The Harlot Babylon		
18. Fall of Babylon		
19. Hallelujah Chorus		
20. Great White Throne		
21. New Heaven and Earth	Beauty, Joy, Life!	**GLORY**
22. "I Am Coming Soon"	Come, Lord Jesus!	

Introduction to the Study

The book of Revelation is one of the most beautiful and inspiring books in the Bible. Its purpose is to unveil Jesus Christ and to reveal him as the victorious Lord, alive, actively involved in his church on earth, working on behalf of his people, ultimately defeating every enemy, and coming again to bring in a new order and a new world.

This book has been an inspiration to poets, artists, and musicians. It has comforted countless sorrowing Christians with its beautiful pictures of heaven. It has encouraged persecuted, suffering Christians to remain faithful to Christ and even to die for him if necessary. It has brought hope to the discouraged and fainthearted with the certainty that every Christian shares in Christ's victory.

But in spite of the great message of the Revelation, it has often remained a closed book. Perhaps one reason is that fanatics have tried to interpret this book and have given such weird explanations that people have been discouraged from studying it. Perhaps a more common reason for not studying this book is that its symbolic language is difficult to understand; people are afraid of it and decide to leave its study to the few brave souls who dare to venture into its mysteries.

It is true that the Revelation contains many difficult passages and many varied interpretations have been given to this book. Yet, it holds a fascination for people who would like to be able to understand its message. It will be our aim to discover the central message of the book. There will be many questions left unanswered. It is our prayer that no one will be discouraged by the difficulties, but rather that each one will be given renewed courage and hope as we view the beauty and glory of our victorious Lord.

It is significant that the Revelation is the only book in the Bible that begins and ends with a distinct promise of blessing to those who read it: "Blessed is he who reads aloud the words of the prophecy, and blessed are those who hear and who keep what is written therein; for the time is near" (Rev. 1:3).

"Blessed is he who keeps the words of the prophecy of this book" (Rev. 22:7).

Characteristics of Apocalyptic Literature—It will help us to understand the message in this book if we realize that it was written in a distinctive literary style peculiar to apocalyptic literature. Just as other forms of literature, such as poetry or drama have their own distinctive styles, so apocalyptic literature has certain characteristics.

6

The word "apocalyptic" comes from the Greek word, *apokalypsis* which means "disclosure," "uncovering," "unveiling," or "revelation." Thus one characteristic of this type of literature is that it looks into the future and seeks to reveal what has been hidden. An example of apocalyptic literature in the Old Testament is the book of Daniel. The Revelation is the only book in the New Testament which exemplifies this type of writing, although Mark 13 has been called "The Little Apocalypse," and there are passages in Matthew and in 2 Thessalonians which are apocalyptic in nature. The pattern for this style of writing came from a body of apocalyptic literature dated from the last two centuries B.C. and the first century A.D. Some of these writings, such as Ezekiel, Joel, and those mentioned above, are in the Scriptures, but there are about thirty apocalypses which have not been accepted into the body of Scripture.

There is much symbolism in apocalyptic literature both in the use of language and in numbers. Most often these writings emerged during difficult times and were meant to give courage and confidence to the readers. The writing consisted of visions announced by angels who portrayed the unseen world.

The Revelation is a Christian apocalypse and, as such, is different in many respects from other apocalypses. In the first place, John states several times that his book is a prophecy (Rev. 1:3; 22:7, 10, 18, 19). Thus he classes himself with the Old Testament prophets, but uses apocalyptic style. While other apocalypses were essentially pessimistic and saw no hope for this evil world, the Revelation is optimistic in view, for it reveals a victorious Christ who is in this world sharing his victory even now with his people.

One writer says, "But clearly, he (John) has not set himself to write just another apocalypse. . . . While it has connections with apocalyptic it is yet different. It is a Christian writing setting forth what God has done in Christ and what he will do, and using something of the apocalyptic method to bring all this out. But the emphasis on 'the Lamb as it had been slain,' i.e. on a past event of history, is both central to Revelation and absent from apocalypses." [1]

Authorship—The writer identifies himself simply as John. Nowhere in the book does he claim to be the apostle. The early church fathers, however, held that the author was John the apostle, who also wrote the Gospel of John and 1, 2, 3 John. The author states that he received the message of the book while he was on the island of Patmos (Rev. 1:9). Irenaeus writes that the Apostle John was arrested under the persecutions of the Roman Emperor Domitian and was banished to the island of Patmos, where the Roman government had a penal colony to work the mines.

However, there are many commentators who do not believe that the author is John the apostle. Because the style, content, and the Greek are so different from that of the gospel, they believe that someone else by the name of John wrote the Revelation. It is well to remember that the source of this book is God (Rev. 1:1) and that the message of the Revelation comes to us through John's pen.

Date—Tradition places the date of the Revelation in the last part of the first century, 95 or 96 A.D., towards the end of the reign of the Emperor Domitian.

Title—As stated above, the term *Revelation* comes from a Greek word which means disclosure or unveiling. This book reveals Jesus Christ and in this book we see him as we have never seen him before. When God came to this earth in the person of Jesus, his glory was veiled in human flesh. But here in the Revelation, this glory is unveiled and in the visions given to John we see the full deity, majesty, and victory of the resurrected, glorified Lord.

Note that the term Revelation is always used in the singular, never in the plural. "Revelations" is often heard. Note how the title is written in your Bible.

This book is the record of *the* Revelation of the victorious Christ to John.

Historical Setting—The book was written at a time of great suffering, persecution, and hardship for Christians. Emperor worship had been growing in the Roman Empire and in the reign of Emperor Domitian (81-96 A.D.) it had reached its peak. Domitian demanded that he be worshiped as God and that he be addressed as "Lord and God." Christians and Jews who refused to do this were called atheists. Some were put to death; others were pressured socially and economically. John looks beyond the immediate persecution to the persecutions which Christians will have to endure throughout all history. The Lord's word to all suffering Christians is, "Cling to Christ! Be faithful to him even if it means death, and you will be rewarded with the victorious crown of life."

Methods of Interpretation—There are four main theories as to how the book should be interpreted:

1. **Preterist**—This theory holds that the book was *written exclusively for first century Christians* and is only of literary interest for succeeding generations.

2. **Historical**—This view holds that the Revelation is a *prophecy of all church history* from its beginning to the return of Christ. This view holds that events and predictions have been, and are being fulfilled at various stages of world history.

3. **Futurist**—This method of interpretation looks on the Revelation chiefly as a *prophecy of future events*. Just as the Old Testament prophets often blended present events with the immediate future and the final day of the Lord, so the moderate futurist sees the immediate judgments

(persecutions under the beast, Rome) as a prelude to judgments at the end of the age.

4. **Idealist**—This theory asserts that the book does not deal with *events,* but gives a *symbolic portrayal of the struggles* through which the church universal must pass—the struggle between good and evil. Thus the message of the book is spiritualized.

What View Shall We Take in Our Study?—Since there are strengths and weaknesses in each of these views, we need not be bound by any one of them. We know that parts of the Revelation were fulfilled in the first century. As we study this book we will see that it has meaning for our day and is being fulfilled even now. But we believe that it is also eschatological in nature; that is, it speaks of the last days relating to Christ's coming again.

Use of Symbolism—One might describe the Revelation as a moving picture on a wide-angle screen with four-channel stereophonic sound and dazzling color! All the symbols, visions, and imagery are meant to get us involved—to get us to respond so that we will not be merely spectators. We must be careful not to be so concerned about the details of the symbolism that we miss the central message it seeks to convey.

Some writers have suggested that one of the reasons for the use of symbolism was to confuse the Roman antagonists. Christians, on the other hand, would understand this code language because its symbolism was rooted in the Old Testament. The more familiar one is with the Old Testament, the better one will be able to understand the Revelation.

The Use of Numbers—The symbolic use of numbers plays an important role in the Revelation. Dr. Donald Richardson and Dr. Julian Love in their commentaries suggest the following meaning of numbers:

3 represents the spirit world, either the trinity of evil or the Holy Trinity. 7 is the complete or perfect number.

3½ is half of the perfect number and is therefore evil. 3½ years is the same as 42 months or 1260 days.

4 is the number of the earth, for example, the 4 seasons, 4 corners of the earth, etc.

6 is one less than seven, therefore incomplete and evil. The greatest degree of evil is found in the number 666 (Rev. 13:18).

10 is a round number signifying all or enough.

12 is a complete number and is seen as sacred like 7.

1000 is the symbol of highest completeness, used at least 20 times in the Revelation.

Some Pitfalls to Avoid—There are many books on the market today which claim to have most of the answers to the mysteries of the Revelation and the end time. Many of the writers can identify clearly in Revelation the role of Russia, China, the Common Market, and other contemporary events. These books may be interesting to read, but they tend to interpret the symbolic language of the Revelation literally and thus satisfy a curiosity about the end times. This is not the purpose of the Revelation.

Christians will keep alert to contemporary events in the world and will follow Jesus' injunction to watch the times and the seasons. But they will remember that God alone holds the answers to the mysteries of the end of the age. Therefore, it is wise to approach this study with an open mind and humility, refusing to let any speculation about the end of the world rob one of the message of hope in this book.

The Message of the Book—The purpose of the book of Revelation is to bring comfort, encouragement, and hope to the church of Jesus Christ in its conflict with evil. The book was written to suffering, persecuted Christians in the first century, but its message is for afflicted believers of all ages. The church of Christ will always be plagued by imperfections, heresies and apostasies; it will be persecuted and tested; there will always be a conflict between the church and the world, between Christ and Satan.

But God is *for* his people and encourages them to live faithfully in this tension between good and evil. Throughout history, God in his mercy permits and sends judgment on the unbelieving world in an effort to bring them to himself. These judgments are symbolized in the Revelation by three series of judgments: the seals, the trumpet judgments, and the bowls of wrath.

Often it seems that Satan is winning the battle, but Christ is in control. When he comes again he will defeat every enemy and manifest his victory to the world. Therefore the Christian may be filled with courage and hope, for the victory of Christ is his now. That victory will be his fully when he stands with his Lord in the new Jerusalem, singing the song of victory with all the saints, "Hallelujah! He is Lord of lords and King of kings."

I. THE VICTORIOUS LORD IS ALIVE

(Revelation 1)

We are introduced to the first vision of the book. What a beautiful vision it is! The Holy Spirit would impress on our hearts that Jesus is alive, that he is in the midst of his church, and that he is the all victorious one. If we keep the certainties of this vision before us, we will be strengthened with courage and hope even in the midst of the judgments which will be revealed in subsequent chapters. But before seeing this glorious vision of Christ, we are introduced to the author, promised a blessing for studying this book, and given a greeting from the triune God.

THE PROLOGUE (Rev. 1:1-8)

The Author and the Promised Blessing (1:1-3)

It is made clear at the beginning of this book that God is the source of the Revelation and that Jesus is the agent through whom the message came to John and through him to the churches. The reader should realize that a book such as this, with its visions and prophecies of judgment and final victory, is not merely human speculation but is in truth the Word of God. Only then can it be believed and trusted.

The words, "what must soon take place" (v. 1) and "for the time is near" (v. 3), may raise some questions. Perhaps they were written so that every generation will wait expectantly for the Lord. The Old Testament prophets merged the distant future with the present so that they often appeared as one. So the seer here looks down through the aeons of time and tells his readers that the dawn is breaking. The Lord's return is always imminent. We may expect him at any time.

The blessing (v. 3) is the first of seven beatitudes in the book of the Revelation. The promised blessing is for those who read the prophecy aloud in the congregations addressed and also to those who listen to the reading. This indicates that this was not to be a closed book, but was to be read openly. It also indicates that the purpose of the Revelation was to bring a blessing which would be experienced when the message of the book was kept in the heart and heeded.

The Greeting (1:4-5a)

The book was written as a letter and used the customary letter form of that day, giving the writer, the reader, and the salutation. The writer refers to himself simply as John, indicating that he was very well known to the churches of Asia Minor.

He addresses his book to the seven churches of Asia Minor. These were actual churches with which John was acquainted. One may ask, "Why was the Revelation directed only to these seven churches?" Perhaps because there were situations in each of these churches which were applicable to churches of all ages. Also the use of the symbolic number 7, which stands for completeness, would indicate that these messages are for the church universal. Another indication that these messages are meant for all who read them is the exhortation which closes each letter, "He who has an ear, let him hear." The extreme futurists (dispensationalists) hold that the seven churches are not actual, historical churches but that each represents a successive stage of world history.

John gives the usual New Testament greeting of grace and peace. The source of these blessings is the Holy Trinity. God is spoken of as "the one who is and was and is to come" to indicate his eternalness. He is the same yesterday, today, and forever. What a comfort to those going through tribulation! The God who led and preserved his people in times past will do so now and continue to do so.

The seven spirits—This phrase refers to the fullness, completeness of the Holy Spirit. Note that the Holy Spirit is before the throne of God. He has access to all the things of God and Christ so that he can minister them to us (John 16:13-14). This imagery perhaps had its source in Zechariah 4. The greeting is also from Jesus Christ.

Faithful witness—This refers to his earthly ministry and death. Jesus was the faithful, consistent witness who sealed his witness with his blood. His example would be a great encouragement to suffering Christians to be faithful even to the point of death.

Firstborn from the dead—Christ's resurrection assures all believers that they, too, will be raised from the dead. What a comfort for all those who have been martyred for their faith or who have been harassed and persecuted!

Ruler of kings on earth—What a comfort to those persecuted Christians living under a Roman ruler who demanded to be worshiped as God and who appeared to be sovereign—what a comfort to them and to all Christians living under anti-Christian governments! Jesus is the ruler of kings. At present he is at the right hand of God, ruling the nations. When he returns, his sovereignty will be revealed and all earthly rulers will fall down before him and acknowledge that he is King of kings and Lord of lords.

The Adoration of Christ (1:5b-6)

When John contemplates what Christ has done and will do for his people, he bursts into a doxology of praise.

He loves us—Note the present tense of the verb. Jesus' love is constant even in difficult testing times when we are tempted to think he has forgotten us.

12

He has freed us from our sins—What greater proof of his love is there than our redemption at the price of his blood! For the early Christians, when evil was so rampant and the love of God seemed so obscure, how comforting for them to be able to look at the cross and say, "We are loved."

A kingdom and priests—All who have accepted the love of Christ and are living in the forgiveness of sins are members of God's kingdom, and as priests, have free, open access into the very presence of God. When these persecuted Christians would remember who they were—in God's eyes "VIPs"—they would be strengthened to stand up to the God-defying Domitian and be faithful to Christ regardless of the cost.

The Second Advent of Christ (1:7)

The second coming of Christ is a great comfort to afflicted believers, for then all wrongs will be set right and righteousness and justice will rule. We do not know how it will be possible for all people on earth to see him, but God has his own Telstar system. Those "who pierced him" are not only those who caused his death, but all who have rejected him. The tribes of the earth will wail when they finally realize who it is they have rejected. This wailing does not seem to imply repentance for there is no indication in the Revelation that judgment brings repentance on the part of God's enemies.

Some commentators have chosen verse 7 as the motto or central theme of the Revelation. It certainly is a recurring motif.

THE VISION OF CHRIST (Rev. 1:9-16)

Note how John identifies himself with his readers as one with them in their sufferings. This statement seems to indicate that he had been banished because of his faithful witness for Christ, perhaps for preaching against emperor worship. Patmos was an island about ten miles long and five miles wide, sixty miles from Ephesus, where tradition says John had served as pastor. It was Sunday morning and as John walked along the rocky coastline of this deserted island, perhaps he was thinking about his congregation, praying for them and longing to worship with them. But God gave him the greatest of all worship experiences.

John is *in the Spirit*—"John's soul seems to have been liberated from the shackles of time and space. He is taken out of contact with the physical world round about him. . . . He *sees* indeed, but not with physical eyes. He *hears*, but not with physical ears. He is in direct spiritual contact with his Savior. He is alone with God. He is wide awake and every avenue of his soul is wide open to the direct communication coming from God." [2]

It is in this state that he hears a voice of power and authority that sounds like a trumpet, and which instructs him to write to the seven churches of Asia Minor.

On turning to see the identity of the voice, he is granted this glorious vision of the exalted Lord. First he sees seven lampstands, perhaps in a semicircle. In the center he sees a figure bathed in light, one who looks like a man—but who is more than a man. His dress, indicating dignity and authority, is like the dress of the Old Testament priests.

His hair *white as wool* implies deity, eternalness, holiness. His *eyes like a flame of fire* represent the ability of Jesus to penetrate the heart and unmask all sin, sham, and phoniness. Implicit here also is the idea of judgment, for when the love of God has been offended, then holy wrath follows. His feet *like glowing bronze* bring to mind a line from the *Battle Hymn of the Republic*, "He is trampling out the vintage where the grapes of wrath are stored." It may mean that he is coming to bring judgment.

His voice would symbolize "a roaring symphony of power perhaps like the sound of Niagara Falls." (Lilje)

The seven stars may represent a supernatural being such as an angel which is assigned to each church, or it may mean the pastor of each church. These stars are in Christ's right hand. He has authority over them; he cares for them; he protects them. What an encouragement for every pastor!

From his mouth a two-edged sword—Here is a case in point where it would be folly to take this symbolism literally. What is it saying? In several places in Scripture the Word of God is referred to as a sword. The Word of God penetrates like a sword (Heb. 4:12), and like a sword it will destroy its enemies (Isa. 11:4).

His face was like the sun—It is impossible to look directly into the sun without being blinded. One cannot even look at an eclipse of the sun without taking proper precautions. Yet the only way to adequately describe the dazzling glory of the exalted Christ was to compare him with the sun shining in all its strength.

This whole vision of Christ is a mosaic taken from Old Testament imagery, especially from Daniel and Ezekiel.

JOHN'S REACTION TO THE VISION (Rev. 1:17-20)

John had been very close to Jesus during his earthly ministry. But now he sees him after his ascension and glorification. The vision of the exalted Lord causes John to fall prostrate before him. Here was Jesus robed in glorious splendor, the exalted King, coming to search out and heal his church and to bring judgment on his enemies. The vision was not meant to frighten John, but to comfort him. How reassuring the familiar words "Fear not" must have sounded to John who had heard them many times before from Jesus' lips. John was assured by Jesus' words that he was indeed the same Jesus who had lived on earth, who had died and risen again to conquer death and the grave. He was indeed God in the flesh, living to conquer and coming again to judge. A loving touch from Jesus restores John's strength and confidence.

14

This vision would bring comfort and courage also to other Christians who were tempted to discouragement, some of whom would be losing their lives for their faith. This vision would reaffirm and strengthen their faith in the living Christ. He was true man. He knew what they were experiencing, for he, too, had suffered and died. He was also true God and he was alive. In him they would be victorious, whether in life or in death.

OUR RESPONSE

We, too, need this vision of the exalted Lord. Too often we have focused our attention on the Babe of Bethlehem or on the lowly Man of Galilee. We need to see in Jesus his authority and dignity, his holiness and purity, his majesty, his power—the One who is coming back to judge. We need 'to permit his eyes, which are as a flame of fire, to penetrate our hearts and expose any sin or phoniness that may be lurking there. Each of us needs to meditate on his words, "I am alive for evermore," until they strike fire in our hearts with the glad certainty that he is alive for us and that he lives in our hearts. Ask the Holy Spirit to imprint the meaning of this vision deeply on your hearts.

II. CHRIST IS CONCERNED FOR HIS CHURCH

(Revelation 2 and 3)

In chapter one of the Revelation we saw the living, glorified Christ standing in the midst of seven golden lampstands, the first vision of the book. These lampstands represent the seven churches to which the messages in chapters 2 and 3 are addressed. In a broader sense, they represent the church of all ages, for the strengths and weaknesses which Christ points out to the Asian churches are found in the twentieth century church as well.

Note that a pattern is followed in each of the messages. First a description of Christ is given, each title taken from the portrayal of Christ in the first vision (1:12-16). Each title relates in a meaningful way to the conditions in the church which Jesus addresses. Then follows Jesus' analysis of each church with words of commendation, rebuke, and warning. There is no word of rebuke for the churches at Smyrna and Philadelphia and no word of commendation for the churches at Sardis (except for the few faithful ones) and at Laodicea. Each church is given an encouraging promise. In each message Jesus says solemnly to the Asian church and to us today, "He who has an ear, let him hear what the Spirit says to the churches."

MESSAGE TO THE CHURCH IN EPHESUS (Rev. 2:1-7)

Historical Background

The city of Ephesus was the most important and most wealthy city in Asia Minor. With a population of a quarter million, it possessed a thriving seaport and was a busy, prosperous business center. The beautiful temple of Diana, one of the seven wonders of the world, was located in Ephesus. This temple became the center for worship of the Roman goddess, Roma, and also for the Roman Emperor. In it prostitution was practiced as a part of the temple worship and to it escaped criminals would flee for refuge. Because of its importance and wealth it was called the Vanity Fair of the Ancient World. Since all roads from Asia led through Ephesus on the way to Rome where Christians were brought to be flung to the lions, Ignatius called Ephesus the Highway of the Martyrs.

The Church at Ephesus

The church in Ephesus was the most important church in the Asian province. Paul stayed there almost three years on his second missionary journey (Acts 19, 20). His ministry was greatly blessed and, although Paul might not have visited any of the other churches in Asia, all the surrounding regions were touched by the transformed lives in Ephesus. Timothy was put in charge of the work when Paul left, and later (about

66 A.D.) the Apostle John was pastor in Ephesus. Thirty or forty years after the church had been established, John was in exile, writing to his former congregation. A new generation had sprung up which seemed to have lost the warm love and joy that had characterized the first congregation. Outwardly, the church at Ephesus was a model church, "a beehive of activity," absolutely correct in its doctrinal teachings. It would not tolerate any false doctrine.

The Nicolaitans were a religious group that had tried to undermine the teachings of the church. Information on them is obscure. It seems they condoned immorality and idolatrous feasts. They had caused much grief and hardship for the church, but the Ephesian Christians had stood steadfastly against them. Jesus graciously commended the Ephesian church for its zeal and strength.

The Message for the Twentieth Century Church—He Looks for Love.

But all these fine qualities in the church did not fully satisfy Jesus. It is a warm, loving, personal relationship with himself that he seeks. Jesus is even more interested in our relationship with him than in what we do for him. 1 Cor. 13 reminds us of the importance of love. Service without love becomes drudgery. Speaking without love becomes mere noise. Affirming correct doctrine without love leads to harshness, pride, self-righteousness and legalism. Enduring hardship without love makes one bitter and rebellious. Love for Christ is the ingredient which must control and beautify all our relationships, whether they be to others, ourselves, or to God.

We need to be careful lest we become so busy with things of the kingdom that we do not have time for the *best*—abiding in the love of Christ. When the church neglects this, it slips into a mere conventional Christianity. Unless there is repentance and a return to a love for Christ which is as "fresh as morning dew," this conventional Christianity will develop into "pious hypocrisy which leads to stagnation and spiritual death" (Lilje).[3]

Because of the seriousness of this condition, Jesus warns that unless there is repentance, the church will lose its light, unless it recaptures its love of Christ.

THE MESSAGE TO THE CHURCH AT SMYRNA (Rev. 2:8-11)

Historical Background

Smyrna was located about 35 miles north of Ephesus on the Aegean Sea. It possessed an excellent harbor, and was a prosperous city rivaling Ephesus for prominence. Smyrna (known today as Ismir) had remained loyal to Rome and had been granted the privilege of erecting a temple to the Emperor Tiberius in 20 B.C., thus becoming a center of emperor worship. In the city which was famous for its games was a large stadium.

It appears that there was a colony of Jews in the city who sided with the Gentiles and the Roman authorities in harassing and persecuting the Christians. It was this group who some years later (155 A.D.) caused the martyrdom of Polycarp, the bishop of the church in Smyrna.

The Church at Smyrna

We have no record of how the church in Smyrna was founded. If not by Paul, then perhaps it was as a result of his ministry in Ephesus. The Christians in Smyrna were very poor in material goods. It was a real sacrifice to be Christians there, for often as a result of this faith they lost their jobs, their property was confiscated and they were imprisoned and falsely accused by the Jews before the Roman tribunals. These Jews, who prided themselves in their religion and their synagogue, had departed so far from the true meaning of their faith that they had aligned themselves with those who practiced emperor worship. They denied Christ and hated the Christians. Thus, instead of being a synagogue of God, it was in reality a synagogue of Satan.

Jesus' Message to the Church at Smyrna

Jesus begins with his comforting "I know." He is fully aware of their poverty, persecutions and harassment, for he himself had experienced the same. But he does not give the Christians any opportunity to feel sorry for themselves. "You are rich in me," he says. He assures them that the period of suffering would be brief, especially so in the light of eternity, and that he was in control of the period of time. The ten days are not to be taken literally, but are symbolic of a short, controlled period of time.

This would be an encouragement to them to be faithful in the persecutions which were a great test of their faith. Jesus tells them that if they are loyal to him—even to the point of giving their lives—he will give them the crown of life.

Smyrna was famous for its games, winners received a garland or a wreath. Jesus was saying, "Be true to me; do not deny me regardless of the cost, and I will give you a victor's wreath that doesn't fade, eternal life with me." And should they die for his sake they would not experience the second death which refers to eternal death, separation from Christ. Jesus gives no rebuke to the Smyrnian church.

Message for the Twentieth Century Church—He Looks for Faithfulness

Responsible observers believe that there have been more martyrs for the Christian faith in the twentieth century than in the nineteen hundred years that preceded it. Fascist and communist governments have repeatedly sought to crush the Christian church. Countless Christians have been imprisoned or put to death. All this manifests the hatred of Satan for Christ.

Will the church in America be spared the suffering which the church in other lands has endured? If America does not repent and turn to the Lord, can it hope to avoid God's judgment? If suffering should come, would we be able to endure victoriously for Christ? How can we prepare for such an eventuality? Here are some suggestions from *World in Revolt* by M. Basilea Schlink who lived through the Hitler regime:

1. We must be completely dedicated to the will of God.
2. We must resist the advance of the enemy by praying and wrestling

for every person who is threatened so that people may be freed from this trap.

3. We must make a clear decision for Christ and stand against a theology that abandons the substance of the Word of God.

4. We must take our stand for Jesus and be willing to be scorned and called old-fashioned by refusing to compromise.

5. We must overcome fear by learning to trust God in everything, in both small and large matters.

6. We must be willing to give up everything that is of value to us, even the most precious things, if Jesus calls us to do it. Whoever does not learn to trust the Father in all matters large and small today, will despair when the time of catastrophe sets in.

Are we willing to face the possibility of suffering for Christ's sake? Are we willing to prepare for it?

MESSAGE TO THE CHURCH IN PERGAMUM (Rev. 2:12-17)

Historical Background

Pergamum, located about 55 miles north of Smyrna, was perhaps the most impressive of the seven cities. It boasted a library of 200,000 parchment scrolls. The word *parchment* (Latin *pergamena*) derived its name from the city because it was first obtained in Pergamum. The city also contained many temples to Roman deities, the most famous being a white marble altar to Zeus built on a hill 1000 feet high. It was one of the seven wonders of the world. Pergamum also boasted a temple to the god of healing, Askelepias. People from all over Asia came to Pergamum for healing. It was a modern Lourdes. There were two main religious cults in Pergamum, the cult of emperor worship of which Pergamum was the headquarters and the worship of Askelepias, the god of healing. Refusal to worship the emperor was considered treason. It was Satan who was behind all these false religions. So influential was he through these cults that it is said that his throne was in Pergamum.

The Church in Pergamum

Jesus tells the Christians in Pergamum that he is aware of the difficult place in which they are living. He knows the pressures to worship the emperor—by sprinkling a little incense before his image and saying *"Kyrios Kaisar"* (Caesar is Lord). He knows that they are a small, insignificant group looked down upon by the elite because they worship the lowly Nazarene. Jesus commends them for remaining true to him in spite of those difficult circumstances. Many of the Pergamese Christians had come out of paganism so the temptation to give up Christ and return to the old religions must have been very keen. But they had remained faithful to Christ even when one of their number, Antipas, had been put to death for his faith. This is the only information we have about him. Note Jesus' beautiful commendation of Antipas, "My witness, my faithful one." The Greek word used here for witness is *martys* from which comes the word martyr.

19

Even though this church, as a whole, had been faithful to Christ, Jesus had to rebuke them because they had permitted an element that was compromising with false doctrine to remain in the fellowship. The church at Pergamum was tolerating impure doctrine in its midst, and as a result was being influenced by pagan morals. The account of Balaam (Num. 22-25; 31:16) refers to any person or group that compromises with the immorality and idolatry of paganism. It was a temptation for the Christians in Pergamum to take part in the heathen feasts and perhaps even to practice immorality which was an accepted part of some of the pagan temple worship. Perhaps some of them, too, were tempted to compromise by sprinkling a little incense before an image of the emperor thinking it wasn't such a serious matter for they really didn't mean it; in their hearts they knew that Christ was Lord. But Jesus tells them that they must take a stand; they were not to tolerate or compromise with evil. The church must exercise discipline and exclude this element until it had confessed its error. The whole church must repent of its laxity or else Jesus himself will bring judgment on the church. Jesus promises those who resist these false teachings that they will feast with him in glory. The *white stone* has been given various interpretations. It could symbolize victory, free citizenship in the kingdom of God, justification, or an eternal friendship with Christ.

Message to the Twentieth Century Church—He Looks for an Uncompromising Stand for Truth.

In A *Study of Generations,* a two-year study of the Lutherans in America, published in 1972, the team of four social scientists reports the following findings regarding beliefs in the American Lutheran Church: 71% believe that Jesus Christ is absolutely necessary for salvation; 50% believe that the devil actually exists; 69% believe that the miracles of the Bible actually happened, and two out of five Lutherans believe in salvation by works. The church needs an intensive study of biblical doctrine. The deity of Jesus Christ, the doctrine of sin, the way of salvation, the atonement—these are a few of the subjects that need thorough study so that the fuzzy thinking among many church members on these important truths may be clarified. Church members need to know what they believe and why, so that when they are challenged by those who claim to have some special revelation from God, they will be able to test those claims by the Word of God. Those who know what God's Word teaches will be able to help others who are floundering in their search for the truth.

MESSAGE TO THE CHURCH IN THYATIRA (Rev. 2:18-20)
Historical Background

The city of Thyatira was the least important of the seven cities. However, it was a thriving trade center with many trade guilds. There were guilds for the potters, cobblers, tanners, weavers, etc. Lydia, whom Paul met in Philippi, was a business woman from Thyatira who obtained the famous purple dyed wool from Thyatira and sold it in Philippi. Perhaps she was a representative of the dyers' guild. Each guild had its god. All this presented a difficult problem for the Christians for if they wanted to hold a job, they were expected to be a member of a trade guild and attend its festivals. This would mean a feast, at which food which had been offered to the guild god was served. Following the feast there usually was much revelry and even immorality. If a Christian refused to be a member of the guild he jeopardized his job and if he walked out on the wild party he was ridiculed and persecuted.

The Church at Thyatira

We do not know who founded the church at Thyatira, but after Lydia had become a Christian through Paul's ministry and returned to Thyatira on a business trip, surely she was eager to tell of her new-found faith. Now she was on the King's business. Perhaps through her witness, many came to know her Lord. These new Christians may have been the nucleus for the church in Thyatira which was growing in the Lord. They were working, loving, and faithfully enduring. Jesus gave this church a finer commendation than he gave Ephesus, for Thyatira had love to motivate its service. But as in Pergamum, this church was tolerating evil.

The Old Testament Jezebel was the foreign wife of Ahab who persuaded her husband to build a temple to Baal, thus corrupting Israel's worship of the true God. Her name symbolizes seduction to idolatry and immorality. The Jezebel whom Jesus named, evidently was a woman in the church who claimed to be a prophetess who had received special revelations from God. This, she said, gave her the authority to teach and advise the Christians. Perhaps she told them that she had the answer to their dilemma as to whether they should drop out of the guilds and thus lose their jobs and suffer hunger and persecution, or remain in the guilds and take part in their unchristian activities. Perhaps she counseled them to stay in the guilds and take part in the feasts and immoralities. This, she said would make them stronger Christians. "In fact," she may have said, "If you're really going to be able to fight sin, you've got to experience it." This was the basis of the philosophy of the Nicolaitans and of the Gnostics. They contended that all matter was evil; only the spirit was good. So one could sin as much as one pleased with the body; it could not touch the soul. Perhaps Jezebel claimed that her revelations were the "deep things of God." But Jesus labeled them the "deep things of Satan."

The church was aware of this woman and her false teachings in their midst, but they did nothing about it. This was their sin. Jesus graciously had given her time to repent. He warned that if she refused to repent she would be stricken with illness, and her spiritual children who had heeded her teachings and committed spiritual adultery would suffer the same fate, spiritual death. There evidently were some who were struggling with her teachings but had not fully become her "children." Their judgment was not as severe. They would suffer persecution unless they repented. The news of this judgment at Thyatira would spread to surrounding churches and would be a warning to them that Christ was

21

aware of anything that they were harboring which was contrary to his Spirit. Jesus concludes with a gracious promise for those who are willing to pay the price of living holy, separated lives. They will share Christ's rule in heaven and will be given Christ himself, the morning star. They will share his authority and his glory.

Message to the Twentieth Century Church—He Looks for an Uncompromising Stand Against Evil.

A church may appear to be successful and growing, like the church in Thyatira, but like that church, too, it may be infected with the spirit of the world. Isn't one of the dangers facing the church today the temptation to be influenced by current non-Christian ideas relating to morality and sex, divorce, alcoholism, racism, power, prestige, etc.? Someone has likened the church to a ship sailing in the ocean. As long as the ship is in the ocean it can fulfill its function. But if the ocean gets into the ship it will mean disaster. So too, if the spirit of the non-Christian world floods the church it will sink.

Jesus is warning the church today that unless its laxity in relation to all forms of sin is firmed up, there will be judgment. The individual Christian needs to examine his own life-style. Are you taking a firm stand against that which the Word of God declares is sin, or are your views being conditioned by the hard sell of the world?

MESSAGE TO THE CHURCH IN SARDIS (Rev. 3:1-6)

Historical Background

Sardis at one time had been one of the greatest cities in the world, but now it was basking lazily in past glory. It was famous for its woolen manufacturing and, according to some authorities, it is thought that wool dying was even invented there. The city was located high on a mountain so that it was almost inaccessible. Because it regarded itself as impregnable and so had failed to keep watch, it had been captured twice by surprise attacks. The people of the city were characterized by a love of ease, luxury, wealth, and profligacy. The city was zealous in promoting emperor worship.

The Church in Sardis

This church had a good reputation and outwardly it had all the marks of an actively alive church. But Jesus' verdict concerning the church was that it was dead. Perhaps it had all the forms of church life—worship, prayer, service—but these were all empty shells. There seemed to be no heresy in the church, no persecution or suffering. It was so dead that there was nothing for which to attack it. It was so lifeless that the community paid no attention to it. Most of its members were nominal Christians, outwardly religious but with no inner reality. As Jesus looked through the facade, he did not find any of their works perfect—that is, complete or adequate. The works were empty because they were not motivated by the Holy Spirit. The description Jesus used for himself in addressing this church assured them that he had the fullness of the Holy Spirit and was able to fill their empty forms with reality.

22

He warned them that unless they repented, woke up to their condition, confessed their hypocrisy and asked the Holy Spirit to fill them, the lights in their lampstand would go out. He would come unexpectedly and they would lose out because they were not prepared. People in Sardis knew the cost of not being watchful. However, there were a few people there who were alive in Christ and shining as lights in the darkness. Jesus knew their names. He concluded with a gracious promise of their future in glory. Jesus gave no commendation to this church, except to the few faithful ones.

Message to the Twentieth Century Church—He Looks for Spiritual Life

What a tragic indictment against a church that seemed so successful and which had a reputation for being alive. "You are dead," Jesus said. As Jesus walks in the midst of the church today does he find areas of outward form which are devoid of inner meaning? In our daily life of faith and worship we all sense an emptiness at times. But are we to discard these forms because they seem empty? No, Jesus says. Fill them full of meaning. If we confess our lethargy and ask the Holy Spirit to fill our lives with himself, he will enable us to respond to every opportunity for service and worship with gladness and thanksgiving.

MESSAGE TO THE CHURCH IN PHILADELPHIA (Rev. 3:7-13)

Historical Background

Philadelphia was the youngest of the seven cities. It had been founded for the purpose of spreading Greek culture and the Greek language to Lydia and Phrygia. Sir W. M. Ramsey says of Philadelphia, "It was the center for the diffusion of Greek language and letters in a peaceful land and by peaceful means." Jesus makes use of this bit of history when he says to the church in Philadelphia, "I have set before you an open door" — for the diffusion of the gospel. This city was completely destroyed by an earthquake in 17 A.D. because shocks continued to shake the city. Many people moved. Others stayed because of the good soil for growing grapes and eventually rebuilt the city.

The Church in Philadelphia

Jesus gives the tenderest and the highest praise to this church. He finds nothing for which to rebuke it. The church may have been small with few resources (little power) but it had remained faithful to Christ. The problem for the Christians here was not the pagan authorities who demanded emperor worship; it was the Jews who had rejected Christ and therefore hated the Christians because they were proclaiming Jesus as the Messiah. For the second time in these letters Jesus refers to these unbelieving Jews as the synagogue of Satan. Through them the devil was pouring out his venom on the Christians.

The open door may refer to the fact that the Christians have the door into the kingdom, Christ himself, who said he was the door. The Jews claimed they alone had access to God. Or the door may refer to opportunities this church had for witnessing to the hostile Jews.

Some of the Jews would respond (bow down) and confess Jesus as their Messiah. But there would be much persecution from the hostile Jews. Jesus promises that he would keep them in the hour of trial. This trial may mean an impending persecution or it may refer to the severe persecution just prior to Christ's return. He would sustain them and give them strength to be faithful. The promise of his coming would bring comfort and encouragement to them. The following statement was quoted often by early Christians, "A lifetime of faith will be of no advantage unless you prove perfect to the very last." The Christians at Philadelphia had been weak and insignificant in the eyes of the world. Because of the earthquakes, they had to move often; because of the persecutions of the Jews, they had to suffer much. Now Jesus promises that once inside the heavenly home, they would be pillars—a symbol of strength and security. There would be no more moving. Christ would write his name on them, denoting ownership. They would be his forever!

Message to the Twentieth Century Church—
He Looks for a Vital Program of Evangelism

God has set many open doors before the church in our day, and the church has gone through those doors into missions overseas, missions at home, programs of evangelism, various forms of social service to those in need. There is some encouragement today, for example, the Jesus Movement in which thousands of young people have turned to Christ, the renewed interest in the Holy Spirit, and a renewed concern for witnessing. Constructive efforts are being made for social reform and for strengthening the structures for justice.

The church must always be alert for open doors. God will open the doors but the church must be ready to go through them. Jesus' word to the church today is, "Work while it is day. The night comes when no man can work." As individuals, we need to be alert to opportunities of sharing Christ.

MESSAGE TO THE CHURCH IN LAODICEA (Rev. 3:14-22)
Historical Background

The last of the seven cities was undoubtedly first in its own eyes. It was a wealthy commercial center, located strategically where three main highways converged. It was famous for the black carpets and garments woven from the soft wool of black sheep. It was a banking center and it is said that Cicero transacted his business in Laodicea. There was also a medical school in the city which had developed a remedy for weak eyes. Near the city were some medicinal hot springs. The city also boasted a gymnasium equipped with baths. Laodicea was the home of millionaires, evidenced by the fact that when in 60 A.D. it was destroyed by an earthquake, it refused financial aid from the government to assist in rebuilding the city.

The Church in Laodicea

It is thought, from reference to Laodicea in Colossians 4:12-16, that

24

the church was founded by Epaphras, one of Paul's converts in Ephesus. Paul evidently wrote a letter to Laodicea from Rome (Col. 4:16) but the letter has been lost.

Of all the seven churches, this one is condemned most severely. There is not one word of praise. In Sardis there were at least a few who had remained faithful but here the whole church came under the rebuke of Christ. This church existed in an affluent society and evidently was itself very prosperous and self-sufficient. Its members were perhaps active in the community; outwardly this church seemed to be in good condition and very respectable. Christ mentions no heresies or sins. But Jesus' severe indictment is that it is neither hot nor cold. In the Greek these words mean *freezing* and *boiling*. The church members had not openly rejected the gospel. They listened but there was only half-hearted response. There was no zeal, warmth, ardor, enthusiasm, or urgency. They were lukewarm. Nowhere else in the Bible does Jesus express disgust as he does here because of this nauseous condition.

There is no one more difficult to win than the person who is self-satisfied, complacent, and blind to his own condition. It is easier to win the "cold" heathen, who have never been touched by the Gospel. Jesus said that harlots and tax collectors would come into the kingdom before the proud, religious Pharisees.

Notice the words that Jesus used to describe this church that was so proud, complacent, smug, and self-satisfied. "You are wretched, pitiable, poor, blind, naked," he said. In spite of their woolen garments, eye salve, and banks they were spiritually bankrupt. Jesus loved this church as much as the others and gave them loving counsel as to how they could secure spiritual clothing, sight, and wealth from him. There were two steps to their recovery: repentance (Rev. 3:19) and faith (Rev. 3:20). These verses spell hope not only for the Laodicean church but for every church or individual who is sleeping in a spiritual stupor. To those who respond and permit Christ to come in and make them alive and rich in him he promises victory.

Message to the Twentieth Century Church—
He Looks for a Burning Zeal

The twentieth century church faces the same problems and temptations as the Laodicean church. We, too, are living in an affluent society. We have beautiful buildings, efficient organizations, thriving, working congregations. Our great danger is that we, too, become self-satisfied and lukewarm, letting the world "squeeze us into its mold." The remedy is to follow the two steps: repentance and faith. When we face ourselves in the light of Christ's penetrating examination, admit his diagnosis, are open and honest about our self-sufficiency and lukewarmness, and repent, then we are ready to receive greater blessings. When we invite Christ in to take control of our lives and make his word and prayer the center of our individual and church life, he will change us from lukewarm Christians into zealous, empowered servants.

III. CHRIST HOLDS THE WORLD'S DESTINY IN HIS HANDS

(Revelation 4 and 5)

In the first vision of the book (Revelation 1) we saw the exalted, glorified Lord standing in the midst of his church, encouraging, exhorting, warning. In Revelation 4 and 5 the second vision is revealed. The scene shifts from earth to heaven and we see God on the throne of the universe and Jesus, the Lamb, holding the scroll of destiny. As this scroll is unrolled we see unfolding in succeeding chapters the intense struggle between the church and the world, between Christ and Satan. We see God's judgments on all who reject him and the final consummation of the kingdom of God. The visions in these first chapters are meant to give confidence and courage to the tried and tested people of God to remain faithful to their Lord.

GOD IS ON THE THRONE OF THE UNIVERSE (Revelation 4)

Again John is in the spirit, seeing not with physical eyes and hearing not with physical ears. A door is opened so that John in his ecstatic state is able to see all the glory and beauty of heaven. John recognizes the voice which calls him to behold this second vision as the same voice which spoke to him before.

The first thing that meets his eye is the throne, the symbol of power and authority. John does not identify the One on the throne but from what he sees he knows it is God, the Father. The reflections of light from the precious stones, the thunder and lightning symbolize the brilliant radiance of the glory and majesty of God. Some interpreters have seen meaning in the colors of the gems. The translucent beauty of the jasper, which some believe to be the diamond, would indicate God's holiness, the brilliant red of the carnelian, his judgment, and the green in the rainbow, his mercy and faithfulness to his promises.

John sees groups of attendants surrounding the throne. First are the 24 elders. Many interpreters believe that they represent all the redeemed of mankind made up of both the Old and New Testament saints (24 symbolizing the 12 tribes of Israel and the 12 apostles). They are dressed in white, symbolic of Christ's righteousness, seated on thrones, wearing golden crowns on their heads. Their struggles are over and now they are victors, rejoicing in the presence of God.

Another interpretation holds that the 24 elders are angels, near the throne of God, ready to do his bidding. Another view is that they are New Testament Christians who have been "caught up" to be with the Lord. Some who interpret the Revelation very literally believe that there are two phases to Christ's coming: he comes first to gather his church, and later to judge. This literalistic view holds that the words to John

"Come up hither" (Rev. 4:1) refer to the "rapture" of the church when all believers are taken up to be with the Lord. According to this view, everything from chapter 6 to the end of the book is in the future, thus Christians will not go through any of the judgments. This theory is known as the "pretribulation rapture."

However, the words, "Come up hither," are directed specifically to John and do not refer to the church. Ladd says, "The entire question of a so-called "pretribulation rapture" is an assumption which does not command the support of explicit exegesis of the New Testament."

The seven torches before the throne (Rev. 4:5) have the same meaning as the seven spirits mentioned in Revelation 1. They represent the Holy Spirit in all his fullness.

The sea of glass, like crystal, which was before the throne (Rev. 4:6a), reminds us of Old Testament imagery and the vision of God given to Moses and Aaron in Exod. 24:10: "There was under his feet as it were a pavement of sapphire stone, like the very heaven for clearness." This transparent, crystalline expanse before the throne, would pick up and reflect the glowing colors of the stones, the gold and the lights, and thus symbolically enhance the beauty and glory of this heavenly scene.

Four living creatures stand on each side of the throne (Rev. 4:6b-8). It is generally believed that they represent the cherubim, the highest order of heavenly beings. This symbolism is much like that in the visions of Isaiah 6 and Ezekiel 10. The eyes in front and behind and the wings full of eyes symbolize their all-seeing intelligence, swiftness, and readiness to serve and carry out the will of God. Their four different heads like a lion, ox, man, and eagle may represent all kinds of God's creation. They symbolize "everything that is noblest, strongest, wisest, and swiftest in nature."

The four living creatures sing day and night of the holiness and eternalness of God. "Holy, holy, holy, is the Lord God Almighty," they sing. The phrase "is to come" (v. 8b) may express the longing of creation to be set free from its bondage to decay; for when Christ comes again, then nature, too, will be released from its bondage (Rom. 8: 19-22).

Whenever the living creatures sing out their glory and honor and thanks to God on the throne, the 24 elders join them. They fall down in humility, casting their golden crowns before the throne, acknowledging that their victory, joy, and blessedness have all come from the hand of God. Their song is the song of creation, affirming that the sovereign will of God is behind everything that exists.

REASSURANCE FOR DISCOURAGED CHRISTIANS

The purpose of this vision was to draw the eyes of discouraged Christians upward to the throne room of heaven to behold the King of the universe seated in radiant splendor, surrounded by his court of worshiping, adoring attendants. What earthly monarch could claim such magnificence?

The boasted greatness of the Emperor Domitian would pale in comparison. The very words, "Worthy art thou, our Lord and God" were chanted by a royal procession when Domitian made his entrance. Early Christians would easily make the application. For here was One seated above the earth who alone was worthy of praise. He alone possessed all power, although at times to the harassed Christian it seemed that the power of Rome was supreme. Here was the Lord God, the creator of all things, even of every emperor—including Domitian himself. Therefore, oh fainthearted Christians, lift up your hearts! Behold your sovereign God. He rules the world from his throne in heaven. He is in perfect control. When earthly rulers boast and strut and make ambitious plans to outwit God, "He who sits in the heavens will laugh; he will be amused by their plans" (Psalm 2). When Domitian demands obeisance, keep the vision before you and whatever the cost, be true to the eternal God of the universe.

Christians who are being persecuted in our world today need the comfort and encouragement of this vision and so do we. As we see atheistic Communism making gains around the world, we need to remember that God is on the throne and that any government that seeks to stamp out the church will ultimately go down to defeat. As we see forces at work which are corrupting our own nation, we need to pray for America, that it may be cleansed and healed.

When discouragement, illness, problems, and unanswered "whys" confront us, we need to know that the God of the universe is in control and interested in every detail of our lives. We need to learn to trust him believing that he cares and that he has the answer. We need to learn to worship and praise him as the hosts of heaven do. Have you learned to praise him right in the midst of your burden or heartache? Try it! Praise lifts the burden. Praise shifts the focus of your attention away from yourself to God. Praise is the highest form of faith, for when you cannot see the answer and yet praise, you are telling God that you trust him, love him, and dare leave the answer to him.

THE WORLD'S DESTINY IS IN THE HANDS OF THE LAMB
(Revelation 5)

Revelation 4 and 5 form a unit; there is one vision encompassing both chapters. In chapter 4 the *throne* held the center of attention; in chapter 5 it is the *Lamb* who has the place of importance.

In the hands of the Father is *the scroll*. This has been given several interpretations:

"It represents God's eternal plan . . . it symbolizes God's purpose with respect to the entire universe throughout history and concerning all creatures in all ages and unto all eternity." (Hendricksen) [2]

"It is God's redemptive plan for the denouement of human history, the overthrow of evil, and the gathering of a redeemed people to enjoy the blessings of God's rule." (Ladd)

"It is the book of the destinies of the world; it contains the record of that which is to happen in the last times; it is . . . the book of history written in advance." (Barclay)

"The scroll is God's redemptive plan, foreshadowed in the Old Testament, by which he means to assert his sovereignty over a sinful world and so to achieve the purpose of creation." (Caird)

All this tells us that God has a purpose for this world and nothing can frustrate that purpose. God's will will be done.

The scroll is completely sealed, and in order for God's purposes to be fulfilled, it must be opened. John weeps that there is no one in all the universe who is worthy to open the scroll. He is comforted when an elder points him to the One who is worthy. The Old Testament references are Messianic promises referring to the victorious Christ. He has already won the victory over every spiritual enemy because of his death and resurrection as the God-Man. He continues to win the victory and at the end of the age he will win the final and complete victory over Satan, death, and every enemy.

In the vision of the Lamb (Rev. 5:6) it is apparent that this picture cannot be taken literally. As in all the symbolism, we must look for the meaning behind the symbol. In the Greek, the word *slain* means "slaughtered with its throat cut." Even in heaven Jesus bears the marks of his death.

The *horns* are symbols of power and authority. The number seven symbolizes completeness and perfection. The *seven eyes* symbolize intelligence and insight. Jesus is the all-seeing, the all-knowing One, filled with the Holy Spirit and possessing all power and authority.

The Lamb takes the scroll from the hands of the Father, reminding us of the words in Rev. 1:1, "the revelation . . . which God *gave him*. . ." The book of destiny is in the hands of the Lamb. Jesus is the only one who gives meaning to history. "In him all history will be consummated" (Eph. 1:10 Phillips). Unless one believes that Christ is coming again to end present history and to usher in a glorious future for the church of God, unless one possesses this hope, then indeed history has no goal and is meaningless.

Social analysts of the day see little hope for the future of the world. Two secular authors, B. F. Skinner, *Beyond Freedom and Dignity,* and Alvin Toffler, *Future Shock,* are joining the many who are asking the question, "Is it too late to do anything about the future of our world?" Both authors offer solutions which are based on naturalistic philosophies. But only Christ has the solution. He alone is worthy to open the scroll and to bring to fulfillment God's destiny for the world. It is his suffering and death that makes Jesus victorious and therefore worthy to open the seals of destiny.

When the Lamb takes the scroll, all heaven bursts into song. First the living creatures and the elders lift their voices in praise to the Lamb.

The elders hold bowls of incense which represent the prayers of the saints. What a beautiful thought! When Christians pray on earth their prayers are backed by all the hosts of heaven, and their prayers ascending to heaven affect the destiny of the world.

They sing a *new song*. The Revelation is a book of new things. A new thing is now to take place as the Lamb breaks the seals of the scroll and thus brings to completion God's purpose for his world. The song is a new one because Christ always brings a new quality into life. In this scene Jesus is crowned with glory and honor because of his suffering and death. He has paid with his blood in order to redeem all men—to set them free from the slavery of sin. To those who have accepted his offer he has given all the rights of the kingdom; they are priests and rulers.

Now the circle of praise grows larger as another group of angels, numbering thousands and thousands, take up the song of redemption. Soon the whole universe is filled with song to the One on the throne and to the Lamb. What a glorious service of worship!

LEARN THE MEANING OF TRUE WORSHIP

Many artists and musicians have been inspired by the beauty of this and other scenes from the Revelation. If possible, listen to a recording of "Worthy Is the Lamb" from the *Messiah*. Page through any hymnal and notice how many hymns have been inspired by the Revelation. Note especially hymns from the sections titled *Saints' Days—Minor Festivals* and *Commemoration*.

Ponder the lessons we can learn about worship from these heavenly scenes. All worship is directed to God, the Father, and Jesus, the Redeemer. Music and singing play a very important part in worship. True worship honors God for who he is and for what he has done. The worship of heaven is joyful, exuberant, beautiful, blended into perfect harmony by the fullness of the Holy Spirit. He will teach us to worship as the hosts of heaven do.

> *Holy, holy, holy! all the saints adore thee,*
> *Casting down their golden crowns around the glassy sea,*
> *Cherubim and seraphim falling down before thee,*
> *Which wert, and art, and evermore shalt be.*
>
> —Reginald Heber, 1783-1826

IV. GOD KEEPS HIS OWN SECURE

(Revelation 6 and 7)

The readers of the Revelation have been encouraged and strengthened through the visions of the risen, glorified Lord. They saw him in the midst of his church, helping and healing. They listened as he examined the churches, and were encouraged to examine their own lives, to confess shortcomings and sins and to invite Christ in to fill their lives with meaning. Only then would they be prepared to live for him and die for him should they be called on to do so.

In Revelation 4 and 5 the readers were permitted to look into heaven where they saw a scene which would encourage their fainting hearts: God on the throne adored and worshiped by the whole company of heaven, and the Lamb, praised by a universal chorus of worshipers because he alone was worthy to open the scroll. The scroll is about to be opened and judgments revealed.

In the midst of these judgments, the Christian must remember that the scroll and these judgments are in the hands of Christ. God is in control; he will keep his own safe and secure.

THE SEALS ARE OPENED—JUDGMENT BEGINS (Revelation 6)

The drama on the stage of history is about to begin. The four living creatures are given the task of summoning each of the four horsemen who ride onto the earth in rapid succession.

The first rider (Rev. 6:2) has been interpreted in several different ways. Some interpreters believe that he symbolizes Christ because he rides a white horse and wears a crown. Others hold that he represents the Word of God, which goes forth into the world to conquer. Another view is that he represents conquest.

In view of the fact that each of the other three horsemen represents a form of disaster on the earth, it would be logical to view this first horseman also as representing an aspect of judgment. He rides forth as a "Christ figure" and looks very much like Christ as he is depicted in Rev. 19:11-12. This is his purpose—to appear as a would-be savior, and thus through deception to conquer the minds of men with propaganda and promises. Millions of people throughout history – and even in our own day—have been enslaved through this kind of bloodless conquest. This rider reminds us of the man of lawlessness whom Paul describes as the one "who opposes and exalts himself against every so-called god or object of worship, so that he takes his seat in the temple of God, proclaiming himself to be God" (2 Thess. 2:4).

The second rider (Rev. 6:3-4) is astride the red horse of war. It is interesting to note that "its rider was permitted to take peace from the earth." This does not mean that God approves of, or sends war, but he does use it for his purposes. War becomes a judgment.

The third rider on a black horse (Rev. 6:5-6) carries a balance in his hand which was used for weighing grain. A denarius was worth about 17c and was a working man's wage for a day. The condition described here does not refer only to famine but also to the fact that food was scarce and expensive.

The fourth rider on the pale horse (Rev. 6:7-8) symbolizes death. This death seems to be a result of the sword, famine, pestilence, and wild beasts. Hades (which is interpreted as the grave or the state of immortal souls before the resurrection) follows death to swallow up all those who have been killed by the plagues mentioned. But note that this rider is given power over *only a fourth of the earth.* God limits his power.

As we learn the symbolic meaning of each of the riders, we realize that they have always been a part of the human scene. Since the world began there have been those who have tried to conquer the minds of men with their deception and lies; there have always been wars and bloodshed, often as a result of the conquest by the rider on the white horse. There have always been conditions of famine, scarcity, and millions dying as a result of the disasters represented by the first three horsemen. Jesus seemed to indicate that conditions would be even more severe toward the close of the age (Mark 13, Matt. 24). Dr. Hanns Lilje says, "We understand that at the end of world history there will be an unparalleled conflict, which can only be endured by God's grace."

The fifth seal reveals the martyrs under the altar of God (Rev. 6:9-11). This symbolic vision tells us that just as animals in the Old Testament were slaughtered on the altar of sacrifice and their blood poured out at the base of the altar, so these Christians, through their martyrdom, are really sacrifices to God. They have been true to his Word and have witnessed fearlessly for Jesus. Since "the life is in the blood," their souls under the altar would represent their lives poured out in martyrdom.

The souls under the altar cry out, "How long?" They are pleading for vindication of God's glory, for their martyrdom is really an attack on God himself. This is not a cry of personal vengeance, but a desire that righteousness might conquer and that the kingdom of God might come speedily. They appeal to the sovereignty, holiness, and truth of God who has promised always to vindicate his own. They pray that God would act and reveal his justice by bringing to an end the martyrdom of Christians. God answers by giving them a white robe, symbolic of the victory and blessedness of heaven. *They are told to rest until the number of the martyred is complete,* until all are accounted for and no one overlooked. This does not mean that God has a fixed number who will be martyred, but it does indicate that the end is not yet and that throughout the history of the Christian church on earth there will be martyrs and God knows each one.

The sixth seal introduces a scene which is associated with the end of the world. The graphic descriptions of the convulsions in nature are borrowed from Old Testament references to the day of the Lord. (See Joel 2:31 and 3:14; Isa. 13:9 and Hag. 2:6.) Jesus uses similar descriptions in Matthew 24:29 and Mark 13:24-25. Note that all of nature and every class of men from the highest to the lowest are touched by these disturbances. However, it is the wicked who are filled with terror, for they have rejected Christ and so they try to hide from the *wrath of the Lamb*. This wrath must be understood not as a personal anger of God against the sinner, but "the working out in history of the consequences of the rejection . . . of the Messiah." His wrath is "the consuming passion of his holy love that wills to destroy all that is unloving and untrue." (Torrance) It is the reaction of his holiness against sin. His wrath also shows that God cares. He will vindicate his own. Wickedness—and all who reject Christ and persecute his children—will one day be judged. God has not forgotten his suffering children. The blood of the martyrs calls out to him and he hears. Thus the vision in the sixth seal is an answer to the cries of the martyrs in the fifth seal. Now they are victoriously at rest and comforted by the assurance that God will vindicate them in his time.

GOD'S PEOPLE ARE SECURE (Revelation 7)

The seals have been opened one by one, revealing judgments that increase in intensity and severity so that at the end of the sixth seal one would expect the final judgment and the coming Christ to follow immediately, but there are other judgments which must take place first. The events following the opening of the sixth seal were so horrendous that all men who have not acknowledged Christ as Savior and Lord, all men from kings to slaves, cry out "Who can stand?" Revelation 7 answers this question. There are those who *can* stand. They are God's own, his sealed ones. They are safe and secure in the midst of tribulation, for God has his eye on them and will not let them go. They may be martyred for his sake, but even so they will be safe and secure with him in heaven forever.

Thus before the seventh seal is opened, there is an interlude describing those whom God has made secure. We see *four angels standing at the four corners of the earth,* one each at the extreme north, south, east, and west, ready to let the winds of persecution and tribulation blow in their fury on the earth. But the four angels are restrained by another of God's angels, one who bears the seal of God. God is on the throne of the universe still! A wind can not blow, a calamity can not touch the earth unless God gives his permission. Jesus said that not one sparrow would fall to the ground without the Father knowing it. The chief reason for the staying of these storms of fury was for the servants of God, his children upon earth. Before the final storms of the seventh seal could be unleashed, God would make clear to his children that, come what may, they were secure in him for he had sealed them (Rev. 7:1-3).

What is meant by the sealing of the servants of God upon their foreheads? A seal used on any official document indicated authenticity, ownership, and protection. It was a mark which could be clearly seen, indicating to whomever was handling the document that it was to be respected and treated with care. God's seal on his children is not a mark on the forehead that can be seen. It is an inner, spiritual reality. It is God's Holy Spirit witnessing with our spirits that we are children of God. God sealed us in baptism, claiming us for his own. His word is filled with promises of care, safety, and protection for his children. "I have called thee by thy name; thou art mine. . . . I will be with thee" (Isa. 43:1-2). "Fear not, for I am with you, be not dismayed, for I am your God; I will strengthen you, I will help you, I will uphold you with my victorious right hand" (Isa. 41:10). "The mountains may depart and the hills be removed, but my steadfast love shall not depart from you" (Isa. 54:10). Here are but a few of God's wonderful promises to his children which assure them that they are sealed, that they belong to God.

With Paul we can joyfully affirm, "I am sure that neither death, nor life . . . nor things present, nor things to come, nor powers . . . nor anything else in all creation, will be able to separate us from the love of God in Christ Jesus our Lord" (Rom. 8:38-39). God's purpose in assuring his children that they have been sealed is to give them courage and hope when the fierce winds of calamity, persecution, and tribulation come upon the earth. Even in the midst of suffering they can look up confidently to him and affirm, "I am his; God on the throne is my Lord. His promises are my security; he will keep me the whole way home."

The 144,000 (Rev. 7:4-8) have been given several interpretations. We will consider the two most common views. One interpretation states that the 144,000 represent Jews who have come to Christ through the preaching of the two witnesses (Rev. 11) during the reign of antichrist. However, as Ladd points out, this passage (Rev. 7:4-8) does not refer to the salvation but to the sealing or protection of those who have already been saved. Furthermore, one may ask why Jews only are sealed or spared from martyrdom while a large number of Gentiles will be martyred.

A more common view holds that the 144,000 represent the church universal, "spiritual Israel," made up of both Jews and Gentiles. The 144,000 are mentioned again in Revelation 14 and there they are specifically referred to as those "who have been redeemed from the earth." The fact that only 12,000 from each tribe are sealed may symbolize that only those who belonged to "spiritual Israel," who are truly members of the body of Christ, can have assurance—security—in the midst of persecution. Others may outwardly belong to Israel, the church, but only a personal relationship with Jesus Christ will keep them secure.

The 144,000, as other numbers in the Revelation, must be interpreted symbolically. It means fullness, *completeness*. It refers to the totality of all the redeemed. God knows just how many there are; therefore a specific number can be used. He knows each one by name. He will bring them all safely home to his house some day; not one will be missing.

A vast multitude which can not be counted is described in Revelation 7:9-17. This group and the 144,000 are not two different groups, but are one company, seen from two different aspects. The 144,000 represent the church militant, on earth. The second group is the church triumphant, in heaven.

The vision of the redeemed in heaven (Rev. 7:13-17) is one of the most beautiful and glorious visions in the book. In this group are Jews and Gentiles, some of whom have suffered martyrdom. All are safe in the heavenly home because they have remained faithful to Jesus Christ. Their white robes are symbolic of the righteousness and festivity of heaven. The palm branches speak of the joy of their victory. They *stand* confidently in the presence of the Lamb, knowing that they are there because he has bought them with his own blood and brought them safely home. What a contrast to the picture in chapter six of those who have rejected the Lamb!

The redeemed sing out joyfully and loudly the theme of their song, gratitude, for the salvation which is theirs. They are in heaven through no merit of their own, but only through the grace and love of God in Christ. All the angels and other heavenly beings mentioned in chapters 4 and 5 take up the song. The angels have never experienced salvation, because they have never sinned. They stand in awe at what God is able to do for a sinner—calling him, overcoming his rebellion, forgiving, cleansing, and purifying him so that he is able to stand in the very presence of Christ! Small wonder the angels join in the liturgy of heaven with their sevenfold blessing (Rev. 7:12).

One of the elders asks John the identity of the white-robed throng. John respectfully and graciously asks the elder to answer his own question. What a beautiful answer it is! The multitude of the redeemed from every nation are in heaven because they have confessed their sins and accepted cleansing through the blood of Jesus. They have been faithful to Christ in the midst of the great tribulation through which they have passed.

What is meant by the great tribulation (Rev. 7:14)? One interpretation holds that it refers to all the trials, troubles, and persecutions through which Christians must pass in every age. Others say that the great tribulation is a period of intense persecution and martyrdom of Christians which will occur before the end of the world. Mark 13:19 and Daniel 12:1 seem to point to such a time of suffering.

Perhaps we can interpret the great tribulation as a combination of these two views. For throughout history, many of God's saints have come through a great tribulation and are now before the throne of God. But toward the end of the age, as Scripture seems to indicate, there will be a period of severe testing and persecution (Matt. 24).

Note the past tense: *"have come* out of the great tribulation." Even though John looks at both the past and the future tribulation, he speaks as if it had already occurred. This tells us something about interpreting the Revelation. Time in this book is not chronological; events do not

35

follow one another as dated by a calendar. In all the visions John is very free in his use of time, as related to events and in the use of symbolism. His symbolism reminds us of surrealism or psychedelic art. Since the visions flow so freely, it is difficult to limit them to a specific time or place.

Encouragement for persecuted Christians is the true purpose of this beautiful vision of heaven. Regardless of their harassment and persecution by the non-Christian world, if they continue loyal to Christ, even if it means martyrdom, they may know that there is a welcome awaiting them in the Father's house. They will be in the very presence of Jesus, whom not having seen they have loved; they will see him face to face and will serve him ceaselessly.

The redeemed will be *sheltered by the presence of God* on the throne (Rev. 7:15). The picture here is of God spreading a tent over his own to shelter them. The tense changes to the future here, perhaps indicating that John is visualizing the condition of the redeemed in the new heaven and new earth.

In his presence there will be perfect satisfaction and contentment. No more troubles, trials, or sorrows. The Lamb becomes the shepherd, reminding us of the beauty of the 23rd Psalm. There will be no more crying, for God will wipe every tear from their eyes.

This vision was meant to give comfort, courage, and hope to suffering Christians. It was saying to them, "Remain faithful to Christ; witness boldly for him regardless of the cost, for there is a great future in store for you. It will be worth it all when you see Christ."

> *O happy day when we shall stand*
> *Amid the heavenly throng,*
> *And sing with hosts from every land*
> *The new celestial song,*
> *The new celestial song.*

Wilhelm Andreas Wexels, 1797-1866
Tr. George Alfred Taylor Rygh, 1860-1943
Reprinted with permission.

V. THE PRAYERS OF CHRISTIANS MOVE THE HAND OF GOD

(Revelation 8 and 9)

Apocalyptic descriptions of the end of the age accompany the opening of the seventh seal which introduces the trumpet judgments. The first four seals describe events which have always been a part of the human experience—conquest, war, famine, and death. The events following the blowing of the trumpets are much more serious in nature. Here we see cataclysmic events touching nature and demonic forces invading the world—all a preparation for the final consummation.

PREPARATION FOR THE TRUMPET JUDGMENTS (Rev. 8:1-5)

The seventh seal is unlike the other six, for when it is opened no plague follows. Rather there is silence in heaven for half an hour. All the music of heaven quieted! Why this prolonged silence? Imagine that you are in an auditorium waiting for a famous violinist to begin his concert. The hall is buzzing with the chatter of the concertgoers. Then the artist walks on the stage and lifts his bow to begin. The chattering stops and the people become quiet, waiting expectantly for the concert to begin. Now imagine that this silent expectation lasts for half an hour and you will catch the idea of the picture before us. This silence in heaven intensifies the expectation and dramatizes the seriousness of the judgments to follow.

Another beautiful interpretation of this silence is that God silences all the music of heaven so he can hear the prayers of his saints. The prayers of God's people are heard in heaven and these prayers move God in his governing of the world.

The incense mingled with the prayers may refer to the intercessions of Christ on behalf of his suffering, persecuted church. It is the merits of Jesus which make our prayers acceptable to God. As the prayers rise to God, the answer to these prayers for vindication and judgment on God's enemies comes as fire is thrown on the earth accompanied by thunder, lightning, and an earthquake. We are reminded of the scene when the fifth seal was broken. The souls under the altar, the martyrs, cried out to God for vindication of his justice, and God answered with an earthquake (Rev. 6:9-12). Here God answers the prayers, not only of the martyrs, but of all his persecuted, suffering children by sending the trumpet judgments.

THE TRUMPET JUDGMENTS (Rev. 8:6-12)

The trumpets are grouped in two series of four and three each, as were the seals. The first four trumpets are catastrophies which affect the natural creation, and the last three affect man. The judgments following the opening of the seals were all natural, ordinary occurrences, but with the blowing of the trumpets the supernatural is added. The first four trumpet judgments are similar to the plagues of Egypt. They are partial, affecting only a third of the creation. The purpose of the trumpets is to warn and call people to repentance.

The first trumpet affects the earth and vegetation; the second affects the sea; the third pollutes the rivers or drinking water and the last trumpet affects the luminaries in the sky. It is difficult to analyze the details of the symbolism associated with these four trumpets. Much of it is rooted in the Old Testament; each of the four trumpets is similar to one of the plagues of Egypt. Jeremiah refers to wormwood as being symbolic of God's judgment on his people who have disobeyed him. "Therefore thus says the Lord of hosts, the God of Israel: Behold, I will feed this people with wormwood, and give them poisonous water to drink" (Jer. 9:15). Some of the symbolism may refer to contemporary events of that day. Some commentaries relate the burning mountain which was thrown into the sea to the eruption of Mt. Vesuvius.

Perhaps it is best not to attempt to pin these occurrences down to specific events, but to realize that very serious natural disasters have taken place throughout history and that severe ones will take place in the future. God would impress upon all people that he speaks in every earthquake and flood, in every disaster, calling people to repent while there is still time. While this call goes out primarily to the unrepentant, it seems that the people of God also suffer in these disasters.

The ecologists of our day would perhaps see significance in the four trumpets. They seem to be the prophets of our time. They are the date-setters telling us that unless we clean up our world, it will be uninhabitable within a relatively short span of time. In a recent newspaper cartoon the earth was depicted floating in space, surrounded by other planets. Across the drawing of the earth were written these words, "This planet will self-destruct within 70 years." Under the cartoon was this caption from The Massachusetts Institute of Technology: "Collapse of human society seen if economic and population growth continues."

In June, 1972, representatives of 114 nations met in Stockholm for a UN conference on the human environment. The goal was "to prevent the world from sinking in its own pollution." The four trumpets may not have any bearing on the ecological problem per se, for the trumpet judgments seem more severe and climactic. Yet scientists concerned with the environment have forced the world to face the fact that disaster may overtake this planet unless steps are taken to halt the deterioration of the environment. Are not the voices of these scientists also a warning and a call from God?

THE CRY OF THE EAGLE (Rev. 8:13)

The first four trumpets have now been blown and three more will follow. The cry of the eagle in the midheaven, where all can see it, seems to divide the trumpet judgments into the two groups of four and three. The eagle proclaims three woes, indicating that the next three trumpet blasts will bring in even more serious plagues. The first four were directed at nature, and at man only indirectly. But the fifth and sixth trumpet judgments are directed specifically at man and touch the whole world of sinful men who reject Christ. The woes are aimed at "those who dwell on earth" (Rev. 8:13). This expression refers to people who have made this world their home. They live for materialistic values giving little or no thought to the eternal.

By contrast the Christian sings, "I'm a stranger and I'm a pilgrim. This world is not my home." He does not become so imbedded in the affairs of this world that he forgets that his real home is in the Father's house. It is on those who have refused God's call to repentance and faith that these woes fall. "Sealed" Christians will be spared these plagues (Rev. 9:4 and 16:2).

THE FIFTH AND SIXTH TRUMPETS (Rev. 9:1-19)

With the blowing of the fifth and sixth trumpets, a new element is added, that of the supernatural or the demonic. John sees a star, symbolic of an angelic being, which is given a key to the bottomless pit and permitted to open it. From this abyss, which is hell itself, pour out billows of dark smoke which cloud the air and darken the sun. Then follow swarms of locusts that sting like scorpions. They are not permitted to harm any vegetation but only those who do not have the seal of God on their foreheads. They are permitted to torment only the ungodly, those who have not given their allegiance to Jesus Christ. This torment is for a limited time, symbolized by the five months. The suffering from this plague is so severe that men seek death, but it eludes them.

In Revelation 9:7-11 there follows a more detailed description of these locusts. They look like horses arrayed for battle. An old Arab saying states that the locust has a head like a horse, a breast like a lion, feet like a camel, a body like a serpent and antennae like the hair of a maiden. (Beckwith) The picture reminds one of the plague of locusts inflicted on the Egyptians (Exod. 10:12-15) and also of the invasion of locusts described by Joel. It is said that only those who have lived through an invasion of locusts can realize the horror and suffering of such an experience. Millions of locusts march in rank across the land, eating every vestige of green vegetation in their path, stopping for no obstruction. They go over the tops of buildings and right through open windows and doors. When they fly, the mass of them cuts off the light of the sun and the whirring of their wings beating on each other reminds John of the sound of chariots rushing into battle (Rev. 9:9).

What is the meaning of this symbolism?

First, we note that these are not ordinary locusts, for they come up out of hell itself; they are not permitted to destroy the green vegetation, as do ordinary locusts, but afflict men; they have a demonic leader whose name is Apollyon, which means "destruction." John is describing demonic beings and the torture, darkness, destruction, devastation, hopelessness, despair, and terror which the powers of darkness can inflict on those who follow the god of this world. The description of the locusts in Revelation 9:7-10 symbolizes the deceitfulness of Satan, for he promises victory (golden crowns) and power to those who follow him, but the torture and devastation which he inflicts is much more serious than any actual locust plague.

The fifth trumpet judgment certainly describes the power and destruction of sin in every age. It may also refer to demonic activity at the end of the age. The great upsurge of demonology, Satan-worship, etc. in our day comes to mind as we study this segment in the Revelation. Those who have been drawn into satanic activity and then have later escaped, tell of the misery and degradation accompanying such an experience.

One such is Michael Warnke writing in *Guideposts,* November, 1972. He tells how he was led step-by-step into Satan-worship with its accompanying use of drugs and sex. These become increasingly "unsatisfying, ugly and terrifying." He describes a black mass and the actual worship of Satan. He became a leader or a "priest" in his group and under his leadership on campus the group grew to 1500 in less than a year. This is how he analyzes his experience: "Even in the most crowded meeting I knew our fellowship was not real fellowship, that though we conducted ghoulish ceremonies binding us together, each of us was really utterly alone and in that loneliness, achingly miserable. The one thing that can keep human beings in the long relationship was missing among us: it was a world without forgiveness. It showed up in the staggering rate of suicides among witches and satanists, the numbers committed to mental institutions and the violent wards of hospitals, the utter lack of regret or even remembering among 'the brotherhood' left behind." Through the witnessing love of several Christians he escaped from this snare and found a new life in Christ.

He is just one among thousands all over the world who are involved in occultism. But there are other demons loose in the world today. There are the demons of violence, bloodshed, drugs, immorality, alcoholism, materialism, pride, etc. These all have their origin in the "bottomless pit" and are abroad in the world to torture mankind with their sting.

The eagle in Revelation 8:13 warned of three woes which were to follow. The first of these woes is now past, according to Revelation 9:12. Two more will follow.

The sixth trumpet is similar to the fifth trumpet in that they both bring forth an invading army. However, the locusts of the fifth trumpet are not allowed to kill mankind, only to torture them. But the army of the sixth trumpet is permitted to kill a third of mankind. This, too, is a demonic army, but rather than locusts, as in the fifth trumpet, it is made up of demonic horses.

John hears a voice from the golden altar. This is the same altar mentioned in Rev. 8:3; it is the altar of incense and symbolizes the cry of the saints for God's justice to be shown through the deliverance of his people and through the final establishment of his kingdom on earth. Again we see God answering these cries in the blowing of the sixth trumpet. The prayers of God's people move him to bring judgment on their enemies. Four angels are bound at the river Euphrates. This river formed the Eastern boundary of the land of Canaan, beyond which lived the enemies of Israel, the Assyrians and the Parthians. These four angels represent evil angels and may also be the leaders of the demonic horde. They are released at the Word of God and only in his time (Rev. 9:15). The number of the cavalry is so large that it cannot be counted. John *hears* the number, two hundred million. As with other numbers in the Revelation, it must be taken symbolically. It represents the vastness of God's judgment on the godless civilization. A third of the unrepentant were permitted to be killed as a warning and a call to the rest of mankind.

The description of the horses and their riders, the colors of their breastplates, their heads like lions' heads, the fire, smoke, and sulphur coming out of their mouths, and their serpentlike tails, all serve to describe the terror of these fiendish, demonic monsters. Notice that most of the emphasis is on the horses, not on the riders. It is the horses who have the power to inflict death. This whole scene pictures war. To the first century Christians this huge cavalry may have meant the Parthians who lived beyond the Euphrates and who were a constant threat to the Romans who lived in fear of a Parthian invasion. The Parthians were skilled horsemen. However, we cannot limit this scene only to the Parthian threat or to Babylonian or Assyrian invasions. It perhaps refers to the hellishness of all wars. But specifically, it refers to the period toward the end of the age when God will send judgment on the godless civilization in a last effort to get them to repent before the last trumpet sounds and the final and third woe, the seven bowls of wrath are poured out.

THE CALL TO REPENTANCE (Rev. 9:20-21)

These two verses make clear the purpose of every natural disaster and of every judgment from God; it is to warn people of an even greater judgment to come in the future. It is God's love and mercy pleading with people to repent before the day of grace is over. In the fifth and sixth trumpets God is giving the unrepentant a taste of the terrible judgments which are coming upon the world toward the end of the age.

Does it cause them to repent? Evidently not. They continue to cling to materialistic values (the works of their hands), to their idols which are also the work of their hands, to demon worship which is closely associated with idol worship, to their murders, sorceries, immorality, and thefts. It would seem that those who did not die in this terrible plague would have turned to God and cried out for mercy, terrified because of all they had seen. But instead, they harden their hearts even more. They have become so entrenched in their style of life that not even

41

stark tragedy can shake them loose. These are not only the "in-the-gutter" sinners but they include the cultured, the religious—all, no matter what their calling in life, who have not submitted their lives to the lordship of Jesus Christ.

WHAT MESSAGE DO THESE CHAPTERS HAVE FOR US TODAY?

1. Let us take our praying seriously, remembering that our prayers count with God as he governs the world. Let us join our prayers with those of the oppressed throughout the world, asking God to right every wrong and to bring justice on earth.

2. Let us pray for the Christians in China, Russia, and in other Communist dominated countries, asking God to sustain his persecuted saints and to open these countries for the gospel.

3. Let us pray for our own nation that it will repent of its sins and become, in truth, a Christian nation, witnessing to the world that "in God we trust."

4. Let us guard against any enchantment with psychic phenomena no matter how innocent they may seem. Let us warn our young people of these dangers. The devil is real; he may promise a new "high," but this will end in an eternal "low," if not abandoned.

5. Let us ask God to give us concern and compassion for people who do not know Christ personally. As Jesus wept over Jerusalem, may that same love motivate us to tell people of the beautiful life they may experience in Christ now, and of the future which is in store for God's children. Many are unaware of the judgment which will come on the unrepentant world.

O God of earth and altar,
Bow down and hear our cry,
Our earthly rulers falter,
Our people drift and die;
The walls of gold entomb us,
The swords of scorn divide,
Take not thy thunder from us,
But take away our pride.

From all that terror teaches,
From lies of tongue and pen,
From all the easy speeches
That comfort cruel men,
From sale and profanation
Of honor, and the sword,
From sleep and from damnation,
Deliver us, good Lord!

Gilbert Keith Chesterton, 1874-1936
By permission of Oxford University Press

VI. THE WORD OF GOD WILL TRIUMPH

(Revelation 10 and 11)

It is interesting to note how the scenes in this book shift back and forth from earth to heaven. This indicates how fluid apocalyptic literature is. Because John is in the spirit seeing visions from God, he is not bound by time or space. In the first three chapters John is introduced to his first vision. He is on earth and sees the glorified Christ and hears his messages to the seven churches.

In chapter four the scene shifts to heaven and John views and hears the worship of heaven, the center of which is God on the throne and the Lamb holding the scroll, symbolizing God's redemptive purposes in history. Then follow the judgments as the seals are opened and the trumpet blown. Following the first six seals there is an interlude (Rev. 7) before the seventh seal is opened. Now following the first six trumpets there is another interlude (Rev. 10:1—11:14) before the seventh trumpet is sounded. Again the scene shifts to earth. The central thought in chapters 10 and 11 is the ultimate triumph of the Word of God.

THE UNIVERSALITY OF THE WORD (Rev. 10:1-7)

A dazzling vision is revealed to John. He sees an angel coming down from heaven who is so huge that he is able to straddle the whole universe. His feet are like pillars of fire; his face shines as the sun; he is enveloped with a cloud; the light of his face, shining through the cloud forms a rainbow over his head. His appearance is very much like that of Christ, and some interpreters say that he *is* Christ. But Christ is never called an angel in the Revelation. This is an angel who is very closely associated with Christ and who has come from the very presence of God with a message which is for the whole world. In his hands he holds a little scroll. This is not the same scroll which was given to the Lamb (Rev. 5). The Greek word for "little scroll" may be translated "pamphlet." Because it is small, the meaning may be that this is a limited revelation. But it is open, indicating that the message is to be revealed to the whole world.

When the angel speaks, his voice sounds like the roaring of a lion, indicating that it is loud enough for all to hear, and is spoken with authority.

John must have understood what was said for he was about to write it down when he was hindered from doing so. We cannot be sure what the content of this declaration was, but usually thunder in the Revelation is associated with judgment. The angel swears by God himself that "there will be no more delay." This may indicate that the message refers to the final series of judgments, the bowls of wrath, which will be ushered in when the seventh trumpet sounds. The promise that there will be no more delay is also an answer to the cries of those under the altar (Rev. 6:9-10) and to the prayers of the saints (Rev. 8:4) telling them that God has not forgotten the injustices and the sufferings of his own. He assures them that he will soon vindicate them fully.

This whole scene would encourage Christians to hang on in faith when the fiery trials come. When they are tempted to give up, let them remember that though their suffering may seem to last an eternity, it will soon be over. "There will be no more delay." God will pour out his wrath on his enemies. His own will be vindicated and they will reign with him in the new heaven and the new earth.

THE EFFECT OF THE WORD IS BOTH SWEET AND BITTER
(Rev. 10:8-11)

John was commanded to eat the scroll. It was sweet in his mouth but bitter in his stomach. It was necessary that as a true prophet of God he assimilate and digest the whole Word of God and experience both its bitter and sweet aspects. Only then could he proclaim its message in all its truth and power to others. This is also true for every preacher and teacher of the Word.

If the message in the little scroll contains the announcement of the final judgments, then the bitter part would be the responsibility of proclaiming the judgment of God's wrath on all who reject Christ, and the pain of seeing many spurn this message. The sweet aspect would be proclaiming God's grace in Christ and the joy of seeing people respond and thus be saved from the wrath to come.

Many interpreters say that the angel and the little book refer to the worldwide proclamation of God's Word throughout the entire Gospel age by preachers and teachers of the Word. They have the responsibility of presenting both the law and the gospel, of warning of God's hatred of sin and of the need for repentance, of presenting the way of salvation so clearly that none will be in doubt about the way. Such preaching may cause some bitter reactions.

There are some who do not want to hear about sin and God's judgment on the impenitent. Thus the preacher may be tempted to soften his message to make it more palatable to all. But if he has digested the whole Word of God, then he has a divine compulsion to speak out fearlessly in love. Presenting the gospel of the love of Christ and seeing people respond to this gospel and grow in the grace and knowledge of Christ is indeed sweetness.

In our own experience in the Word there is also the bitter and the sweet. When we digest the Word and it begins to show us our sin, weaknesses, failures, and disobediences, when we realize that we must die to self and let Christ be the absolute Lord of our lives, then we, too, may experience sorrow and bitterness. But if we acknowledge all that God shows us, accept his forgiveness, and grow in our surrender to his lordship, then we will experience the sweetness which the awareness of his presence brings to us.

THE WITNESS OF THE WORD (Rev. 11:1-13)

This passage has been given a variety of interpretations. We will look at three of the most widely accepted interpretations.

Some interpret this chapter literally. They believe that the measuring of the temple (Rev. 11:1-2) refers to the actual rebuilding of the Jewish Temple in Jerusalem toward the end of the age. The altar and the inner sanctuary refer to Jews who come to believe in Christ. The outer court which is given over to the nations to be trampled over for 42 months (or three and a half years) refers to the great persecutions the Jews will go through during the reign of antichrist. During this time two men will be sent from God, perhaps Moses and Elijah or two who come in their spirit. They will be filled with the Holy Spirit and given power to perform miracles. They will preach for three and a half years and, as a result of their witness, many Jews will be won to Christ.

Some who hold to this interpretation say that the 144,000 of chapter seven are the Jews won during this period. These converted Jews will become missionaries to the whole world. After three and a half years of preaching, the two witnesses will be killed by antichrist who is angered by their preaching. Their bodies are left lying in the street; but after three and a half days they are resurrected and taken up to heaven. As a result of the events which followed their restoration and ascension, many people come to faith.

A more common view interprets this passage symbolically. The temple represents the people of God. Paul speaks of the temple of God as being made up of living stones and of each Christian as being a temple for the Holy Spirit. The measuring is symbolic for protection and security and has much the same meaning as the sealing in chapter seven. The inner court refers to true Christians, those in whose hearts the Holy Spirit dwells. They are protected. They may suffer physically but they will be eternally safe. The outer court symbolizes those who are nominal Christians, those who have the outer forms of religion but who lack the inner reality. They are actually a part of the world, have adopted its way of thinking and feel perfectly at home in the non-Christian world.

The 42 months (or three and a half years) symbolize the entire Gospel age from the first coming of Christ to his second coming in glory. The two witnesses represent the witness of the true church throughout its existence in this world and its missionary activity. They are dressed in sackcloth because they preach repentance. They are so filled with the Holy Spirit that their words come forth with the power of fire as they proclaim God's wrath against sin. But the message of the church is rejected by the hostile world, symbolized by Jerusalem which also rejected and killed the Messiah.

Finally, toward the end of the age, the hostile world inspired by Satan, silences the voice of the church. It loses its power and influence and is actually dead. But when Christ comes again it will be raised to life and caught up to be with him. Then the true glory and power of the church will be made manifest to the world. The sight will cause the world to be struck with fear and awe. An earthquake and other awesome signs will precede the final judgment. The world will be amazed and terrorized but it will not repent.

There are variations of the symbolic interpretation of this chapter. Some believe that two actual witnesses will appear toward the end of the age, preaching in the spirit of Moses and Elijah. The Jews of the Old Testament looked for a special messenger to come from God before the end of the age. Malachi identifies one of the messengers as Elijah (Mal. 4:5).

A *third view* holds that chapter 11 tells us about God's dealings with his people, the Jews. Christians have always wondered what place the Jews hold in God's plan and how God will bring about their salvation. Those who interpret this chapter according to this third view believe that this segment answers some of these questions. This view is similar to the first one presented, but it does not interpret each detail as literally as the first.

The measuring is not literal but refers to the preservation of the remnant of Jews who come to faith in Christ, symbolized by "the altar and those who worship there" (Rev. 11:1). The outer court and the city of Jerusalem represent the whole nation of Israel which will be "trampled on" because of its rejection of the Messiah. The 42 months refer to a period of great suffering and persecution toward the end of the age. The two witnesses are usually believed to be actual persons who will come in the spirit and power of Moses and Elijah to preach repentance to Israel. After their mission is accomplished, they will be killed by the beast. The non-Christian Gentile world joins with the Jewish nation in celebrating the death of the two witnesses. Their denunciation of sin and their proclamation of Jesus as the Messiah anger both the Jews and the Gentiles. But the resurrection and the ascension of the two witnesses, and the signs following, cause the conversion of the rest of the Jews.

According to Dr. Hanns Lilje in his book, *The Last Book of the Bible*, Jerusalem is not to be taken merely symbolically. He says, "In some way or other the earthly, geo-historical Jerusalem will have its place in the history of the last days . . . that which God once willed for historical Israel and for Jerusalem will be fulfilled."

Since chapter 11 is considered by most interpreters to be the most difficult in the Revelation and since most commentators do not agree on the interpretation of many of the details, it is best that we also humbly admit that we do not have the answer. However, we will want to keep open and explore possible answers. In our day when we are witnessing thousands of Jews from all over the world returning to the new nation of Israel, we will not write this off as having no significance, but we will ask the question, *"Does this have meaning in relation to God's program for the Jews?"* When we realize that Jerusalem, which has been conquered about 40 times over the centuries, is now again united under Jewish control, we will ask the same question. There are mysteries here to which only God knows the answers. Let us leave them with him and keep alert and prepared for the return of Christ.

Verse 14 states that the second woe has passed. This evidently refers to the judgments following the sixth trumpet. The first woe was the fifth trumpet, according to Revelation 9:12. The third woe, which is soon to come, must refer to the final series of judgments, the bowls of wrath (Rev. 16).

THE TRIUMPH OF THE WORD (Rev. 11:14-19)

The scene now shifts to heaven and John hears the heavenly choirs sing in exaltation because Christ has defeated every enemy and established the kingdom of God on earth. Christ is now the sovereign Lord.

We hear the first strains of the "Hallelujah Chorus" in the words "The kingdom of this world has become the kingdom of our Lord and of his Christ, and he shall reign for ever and ever." This song is sung in anticipation of Christ's victory at his second coming. We will hear the remainder of the "Hallelujah Chorus" in Revelation 19.

In Revelation 1:8 God is described as the Alpha and the Omega, the one "who is, who was and who is to come." In Revelation 11:17, the phrase, "who is to come" is omitted, for in this anticipatory vision, Christ has already come and begun to reign. John, in his vision, looks into the future and sees these events as if they have already taken place. He sees also the final rage of the godless world and the final judgment (Rev. 11:18).

Another encouraging aspect of this vision is the open temple of God in heaven revealing the ark of the covenant (Rev. 11:19). The ark of the covenant was kept in the Holy of Holies in the tabernacle and was seen only once a year by the high priest. It was symbolic of God's presence with his people, and of his mercy. The cover of the ark was called the mercy seat. In this vision, the ark of the covenant is revealed for all to see. No longer will God be hidden, but when Christ comes again, then "He will dwell with them, and they shall be his people, and God himself will be with them" (Rev. 21:3), and "they shall see his face" (Rev. 22:4).

While the ark of the covenant means comfort and the certainty of his presence for his own, to the ungodly world it will mean judgment, terror, and exclusion from his presence, as symbolized by the lightning, loud noises, thunder, earthquake, and hail.

This vision would bring much courage and hope to persecuted Christians. It would motivate them to keep on witnessing fearlessly with the certainty that the Word of God is powerful and that it will accomplish all that God intends. And should their witnessing result in their martyrdom, let them listen to the choirs of heaven singing the "Hallelujah Chorus," proclaiming Christ's victory, and their victory, in him.

47

WHAT MESSAGE DO THESE CHAPTERS HAVE
FOR US TODAY?

1. Our greatest responsibility today is to be faithful witnesses, spreading God's powerful Word to an often unheeding world. First, we must assimilate the Word thoroughly; we must be filled and controlled by the Holy Spirit so that our words will have power; we must be true to the Word of God, witnessing with boldness, knowing that we may experience misunderstanding, rejection, or suffering. Dr. Lilje says: "It is more important to be a witness to Christ, as he himself was 'the witness' absolutely, than to penetrate into the mysteries of the last days. . . . There is no other way to bear witness and to stand up for Christ before the world, than to bear it 'openly,' that is, by suffering. The true follower of Christ cannot evade the way of suffering." [3]

2. When we are tempted to be dismayed because of the seemingly hopeless situations in the world, the vision which John saw will encourage us. We may listen often to the "Hallelujah Chorus" and keep the victorious song of the heavenly hosts in our hearts. Some day the kingdom of this world will become the kingdom of our Lord and of his Christ, and he shall reign for ever and ever. Hallelujah!

3. Jesus has delayed his second coming for many centuries. But the words which John heard, "that there should be no more delay," certainly are more true today than ever before. As we live in the joyful expectation of his coming, this truth will give us a great sense of urgency as we go about the "King's business."

Thy kingdom come! O Father, hear our prayer;
Shine through the clouds that darken everywhere;
Thou only light, thou only life and joy,
Show us the hope that nothing can destroy.

Thy kingdom come, and come thy glorious Son;
O may our task for him be nobly done!
Faithful and true let all thy servants be,
Till they shall bring all nations home to thee. Amen.

—Margaret Rebecca Seebach, 1875-1948
Used by permission

VII. THE DEVIL IS A DEFEATED FOE

(Revelation 12 and 13)

Two series of judgments have passed, the seals and the trumpets. The seventh trumpet has been blown. Two woes have been revealed and a third one is to come when the final judgments, the bowls of wrath, are poured out (Rev. 16). But before this happens, we are introduced to the enemy who is behind all the opposition and persecution of Christians. We have seen the surface conflict between the world and the church. In these chapters we will see the subsurface conflict, the war that is raging between Satan and Christ. We will see that Satan has representatives on earth to do his fiendish work. We will be encouraged to know that the evil one has been dealt the death blow and that victory over him is available to every Christian.

THE BIRTH OF THE CHILD—THE FOCUS OF CONFLICT
(Rev. 12:1-6)

As you read the above caption, you may ask, "Didn't the conflict with Satan begin before Christ was born?" Yes, we saw it in the garden of Eden where God spoke to the serpent about the enmity between him and the seed of the woman, predicting the fatal blow to the devil (Gen. 3:15). It was the birth of Christ which Satan sought to hinder, and it is this fact, his hatred of the Messiah, which this scene seeks to portray. While this account brings to mind the birth of Jesus in Bethlehem, we must remember that it is a vision which John sees in the heavens and each of the figures is symbolic. John goes beyond the historical birth of the Messiah. The woman is a symbolic figure that represents the ideal people of God, the church. She symbolizes not only the Old Testament people of God, true Israel, but also the New Testament people of God. She not only brings forth the Messiah, but is also the mother of Christians (Rev. 12:17). Her glorious description (Rev. 12:1) tells of the beauty and honor which God has given to his people, the church.

There is no doubt as to the identity of the dragon. It is the serpent of Genesis, Satan. He is pictured as a fierce monster. His seven heads and ten horns with seven diadems or crowns depict his great might and universal power. Paul speaks of Satan as being the "god of this world." The red color of the dragon may symbolize the fact that he is a murderer, a destroyer. It is the devil's aim to destroy the Messiah as he waits for the woman to give birth. But he is defeated in his attempt to kill the Child so he pursues the woman who is preserved and protected by God.

The male Child is Jesus the Messiah. John identifies him with the One in the Messianic Psalm 2 who "is to rule all the nations with a rod of iron" (Rev. 12:5). As in other references to Christ in the Revelation,

49

John is not interested in portraying the earthly life of Jesus. Rather he portrays him in his glorified power and majesty. Hence, in this scene, the Child is caught up to the throne of God, symbolizing Jesus' complete victory over Satan. The "catching up" implies Jesus' death and resurrection and his rulership with God the Father.

THE DEFEAT OF THE ENEMY (Rev. 12:7-12)

The war in heaven described in these verses is not to be taken literally. In symbolic language John is telling us that Satan has been defeated. Jesus' death on the cross broke the power of Satan. There are some commentators who relate this incident to the fall of Satan in the words of Isaiah, "How you are fallen from heaven, O Day Star, son of Dawn!" (Isa. 14:12). But here, as in the first paragraph, John goes beyond any point in time. He is affirming the fact that the devil has lost his place of power forever. John does not describe in detail how the defeat took place. Rather he wants every tempted and tried child of God to know that the enemy has been dealt a death blow.

CHARACTER AND ACTIVITY OF SATAN (Rev. 12:9-10)

His name *Satan* means "the adversary." He is against God and Christ, against all that is holy and good. He is the enemy of every Christian. He is also spoken of as the deceiver of the whole world. Jesus said of him, "He . . . has nothing to do with the truth, because there is no truth in him. When he lies, he speaks according to his own nature, for he is a liar and the father of lies" (John 8:44). Notice the scope of his influence; he deceives the whole world (Rev. 12:9). Ponder the countless ways by which Satan is deceiving the world today: false religions which deny the deity of Christ, the fact of sin, the need of a Savior and the cross; godless rulers who attempt to stamp out Christianity; Satan worship and the great upsurge of interest in the occult; the propaganda of the world; the glamour of the materialistic way of life, and the big deception about the devil himself—that he doesn't exist and that anyone who believes in him belongs in the Dark Ages.

He is also described as being the accuser of the brethren. He not only accuses Christians when they fall into sin, but he emphasizes the guilt, keeping the person looking at the sin instead of looking to Christ and accepting forgiveness. Or he may accuse the Christian falsely when he isn't guilty at all, and make him feel guilty. But he was defeated when Christ died on the cross. Therefore a voice breaks out from heaven celebrating this victory. The martyrs defeated him when they refused his temptations to deny Christ. Instead they held faithfully to their word of testimony, counting faithfulness to Christ more important than life itself.

Revelation 12:12b seems to refer to the end of the age, when Satan, knowing that he has little time left, will double his efforts to deceive and capture the minds of men by bringing suffering and persecution on Christians.

ATTACK ON GOD'S PEOPLE (Rev. 12:13-17)

When the devil realizes that, in spite of all his efforts to the contrary, Christ came, died for the sins of the world, was raised in triumph, and ascended to the Father to rule victoriously, he then turns his anger on the woman, the people of God. His initial attack is against the Child, but when that fails, he attacks the woman. But God protects the woman by giving her the wings of an eagle, symbolic of preservation, support, and care. God said to his people Israel through his servant Moses, "You have seen what I did to the Egyptians, and how I bore you on eagles' wings and brought you to myself" (Exod. 19:4). The persecution of the Israelites in Egypt under Pharaoh and God's awareness of their suffering and his loving protection and deliverance of his children out of the hands of Pharaoh really prefigure the experience of Christians in this world. They are living in hostile territory and the devil pursues and persecutes them through other Pharaohs, whether it be a Nero, a Domitian, or a contemporary tyrant. But God is aware of their need and delivers them (Rev. 12:14). And when the evil one spews out his waters of hatred to engulf the woman, God provides a way to escape and a place of security and safety for his children.

When Satan is again frustrated in his attempts to destroy the woman, he directs his attacks against individual Christians, "those who keep the commandments of God and bear testimony to Jesus" (Rev. 12:17). This may refer to the final great persecution toward the end of the age, when Satan, knowing that his time is short, intensifies his efforts to destroy the Christian.

The last verse of chapter 12 pictures the dragon standing on the shore of the sea looking at the beast rising out of the sea.

THE DEVIL'S HENCHMEN (Revelation 13)

The devil does his work on earth through his agents who are devoted to doing his will. Revelation 13:1-10 introduces the first of these, the beast out of the sea. The second beast out of the land (Rev. 13:11-18) is also called the false prophet (Rev. 19:20) and enforces the edicts of the first beast.

THE BEAST OUT OF THE SEA (Rev. 13:1-10)

John, standing on the shore, sees a horrible beast emerge from the sea. This beast is similar to the dragon (Rev. 12:3), for each has seven heads and ten horns. As the beast continues to rise from the sea, John sees its body, fierce as a leopard ready to leap upon its prey, and its feet like bear's feet, able to claw, tear, and destroy. Its mouth reminds one of Peter's description of the devil who "prowls around like a roaring lion, seeking someone to devour" (1 Peter 5:8).

The sea from which the beast rises is said to refer to people or nations. "Ah, the thunder of many peoples, they thunder like the thundering of the sea! Ah, the roar of nations, they roar like the roaring of mighty waters" (Isa. 17:12). The blasphemous name on the beast's head is often understood to refer to the blasphemy of the Roman emperors who claimed divinity and demanded that they be called *Lord,* as did Domitian. Thus this beast symbolizes any ruler or nation which usurps God's place. The Babylonians, the Assyrians, the Roman Empire, down to present day godless leaders and nations all typify the first beast. The nations are symbolized by the seven heads and the kings by the ten horns.

Possible Meanings of the Term Antichrist

Some interpreters identify the beast out of the sea with antichrist. This term has been given several interpretations.

Some believe that *antichrist* refers to the spirit of an age that is anti-Christian, anti-God.

Others believe that the term refers to anything which would usurp the place of Christ in the life of a Christian.

Another interpretation holds that *antichrist* refers to any teaching which obscures or distorts the gospel.

All of these interpretations blended together describe the *spirit* of antichrist.

However, there are some who believe that the spirit of antichrist will become incarnated in a person who will make his appearance toward the close of the age. This view stresses the idea that antichrist will be embodied in a person rather than being merely a spirit or an influence.

The term *antichrist* is used in Scripture only by John in his letters. He says (1 John 2:18, 22), "Children, it is the last hour; and as you have heard that antichrist is coming, so now many antichrists have come. . . . Who is the liar but he who denies that Jesus is the Christ? This is the antichrist, he who denies the Father and the Son." John also refers to the spirit of antichrist as that "which does not confess Jesus" (1 John 4:3). Thus it would seem that John uses the term *antichrist* to refer both to incorrect doctrine concerning Christ, and to people who propagate false teachings.

Some interpreters believe that Paul is referring to antichrist in the following passage: "That day will not come, unless the rebellion comes first, and the man of lawlessness is revealed, the son of perdition, who opposes and exalts himself against every so-called god or object of worship, so that he takes his seat in the temple of God, proclaiming himself to be God. . . . The coming of the lawless one by the activity of Satan will be with all power and with pretended signs and wonders, and with all wicked deception for those who are to perish, because they refused to love the truth and so be saved. Therefore God sends upon them a strong delusion, to make them believe what is false, so that all may be condemned who did not believe the truth but had pleasure in unrighteousness" (2 Thess. 2:3-4, 9-12).

Jesus spoke of false Christs which were to come and of the "desolating sacrilege" which would pollute the temple (Matt. 24:15) and perpetrate a severe persecution of Christians.

52

Dr. Hanns Lilje says, "In every respect the beast seems to be a caricature of the Messiah, as a caricature of Christ he is Antichrist. . . . The beast from the abyss, the symbol of Antichrist, is the most pictorial expression of the truth that the course of history is handed over to this power which fights against God, and that this anti-Christian power will not be overcome within the course of history, but that it will continue to grow, till at the very end of history it will be defeated, and completely annihilated by Christ, to whom all power alone belongs." [3]

As we continue our discussion of this difficult chapter, keep in mind the above possible meanings whenever the term *antichrist* or *beast* are used.

The Reign of the Beast

The beast receives his power and authority from Satan (Rev. 13:2) and uses this devil-inspired pride to blaspheme God and deify himself (Rev. 13:5-6). He is so convincing that the whole godless civilization worships him (Rev. 13:7-8). He makes a last attack on Christians, the worst being his demand for worship (Rev. 13:8). Christians refuse to worship the beast and for this they meet a martyr's death. Thus it seems that the beast conquers them (Rev. 13:7), but John reminds his readers that the death of the martyrs is in reality a crowning victory. God knows each martyr by name and that name has been written in the book of life (Rev. 13:8). They have held to the faith of the crucified Lamb of God and so are safe and secure forever in the Father's house. John also reminds them that God is in control and that the beast would have no power unless it was permitted by God. Therefore whether they are taken captive or killed, they are to accept it and to endure bravely. When things become so dark and painful that it seems the devil has control of everything, God will enable them to persevere in faith (Rev. 13:9-10).

The beast's "mortal wound that was healed" (Rev. 13:3) has been given several interpretations. One relates to Nero who instigated a severe persecution of the Christians in Rome. It is said that he set fire to the city so that he could be honored for rebuilding it. When the whole city discovered his crime, Nero attempted to shift the blame to the Christians, and instigated a series of horrible persecutions. Some Christians were soaked in oil and used as human torches; others were thrown to the lions. In 69 A.D. Nero committed suicide. Later as other persecutions broke out, there was a rumor that Nero had come back to life. During the reign of Domitian toward the close of the century, some believed that Nero was living again in him. Other views assert that the spirit of Nero will live again even more fiercely in another tyrant who will counterfeit Christ even to the point of appearing to die and rise again.

THE BEAST OUT OF THE EARTH—THE FALSE PROPHET
(Rev. 13:11-18)

John sees a second beast, this one emerging from the earth. In contrast to the first beast, this one has only two little horns and looks like an innocent lamb. It does not have the ferocious qualities of the first beast, but when it speaks, its true character is revealed. Its speech indicates that it is inspired by the dragon (Satan). The second beast works in close conjunction with the first beast, getting its directions and authority from him. It enforces the edict of the first beast, that all men worship him, and induces "those who dwell on earth," that is, the non-Christian world, to make an image of the first beast. Either through magic, ventriloquism or the power of the devil, it makes the image speak. This beast is also able to work other "wonders" so as to deceive the non-Christians (Rev. 13:13-15).

The second beast carries out the edicts of the first beast by exercising economic control over people. He demands that they identify themselves as followers of the beast by means of a mark which will indicate their loyalty to him. Whether this refers to an actual mark, we do not know. However, we are reminded of the star of David which all Jews were to wear as a mark of identification during the Hitler regime. The fact that the beast's mark is to be worn on the right hand or on the forehead indicates that it is to be in a prominent place so that there can be no mistaking the person's loyalty. The forehead and the right hand may also refer to the person's thinking or philosophy of life, to his actions, and life-style. In other words, every person is to show in an unmistakable way that he reveres and honors the beast. Christians refuse to do this, thus the absence of the mark indicates clearly to whom they belong. In a sense, this mark is a devilish parody of the sealing of Christians as described in Revelation 7. The sealing was an inward mark of ownership and security. The mark of the beast is also an indication of ownership. A refusal to obey his edict would mean a deprivation of the necessities of life; for the Christian it means death.

The second beast works not only very closely *with* the first beast, but he works *for* him, carrying out his orders. Thus in the first century, under the regime of the Roman emperors who are symbolized by the first beast, the second beast would symbolize the priestly group, the religious system whose job it was to enforce and maintain emperor worship. Throughout the centuries, this beast represents any religious leadership which works hand in hand with a godless government to divert worship away from the true God. This beast is also called the false prophet (Rev. 16:13; 19:20), indicating that his function is of a religious nature. The deception by the false prophet is insidious and subtle because he looks as innocent as a lamb. Think of the millions of people who have been, and are being drawn into false religions through the deceitful pleasantries of the false prophet. Jesus has said that the devil fashions himself as an angel of light.

The Number of the Beast

There has been much speculation as to the meaning of the number 666 by which the beast was to be recognized. John is using a device known to the Jews as gematria. The Greeks used this method also. In the ancient world the Greeks and Hebrews used the letters of the alphabet to represent numbers. Thus a name could be converted into a number. The following example of graffiti has been found on the walls of Pompeii: "I love her whose number is 545" (Caird). Using this method, people have tried to determine the identity of the beast. Many names have been suggested including Nero and Hitler.

If one agrees with the position of Richardson and Love that six is an incomplete number and implies evil, then we may arrive at a better understanding of the meaning of 666. The beast may try to counterfeit Christ by exerting demonic power and demanding to be worshiped, but he will always be a number 6, imperfect, incomplete, evil. He will never attain to number 7 even though he extends himself to a million sixes. The three sixes may also imply a trinity of evil. The fact that it is a human number (Rev. 13:18) may indicate that he will never be divine, and also that antichrist may be a human being.

Practical Lessons from These Chapters

One of the main truths from these chapters is the certainty of the existence of a *personal* adversary, the devil. Nowhere in Scripture is he referred to as an *impersonal* being or an influence. Jesus always referred to Satan as a person, using the pronoun *he*. One of the subtle lies of the devil is to cause people to believe that he does not exist at all, or to believe that he is merely a bad influence or evil, in general. (C. S. Lewis in his *Screwtape Letters* gives helpful insights into the duplicity of Satan.)

Another important fact is that Satan is a *defeated* enemy. What an encouragement to suffering Christians when going through the fires of persecution to know that though the devil does his worst, God has the last word and is in ultimate control. God will provide a way of escape.

What are some ways by which the devil seeks to defeat Christians? He tries to implant lies in the mind by saying, "You haven't really sinned," or "Your sins are too great for God to forgive." If a person has confessed his sins and asked for forgiveness, the enemy may bring them back to mind and say, "You're not really forgiven." Satan may try to implant lies about God and about the person and work of Jesus Christ. He may try to inject feelings of discouragement, depression, or even neuroses with thoughts about illness and death. He will use any means to harass the Christian and take away his peace.

How many Christians live a life of victory over the enemy? First we must be aware of his tactics. The Word of God tells us we are not to be ignorant of his devices. Much that plagues the Christian is from the evil one. Like Jesus, we must use the Word of God against him. Though it may not be applicable in every situation, the following is an illustration of how one Christian found release through the power of Christ:

"At a retreat one Saturday evening we were discussing this matter of victory over the enemy. The next morning a woman told of her struggle with vile thoughts which plagued her whenever she was about to receive the Lord's supper. She had prayed about this, blaming her sinful nature, but found no release. That morning, before the service of Communion, the disturbing thoughts returned. This time she prayed differently saying, "If these thoughts are from Satan, I refuse them in the name of Jesus and by the power of his blood." She stated that she was released and was able to commune with a glad and peaceful heart.

When there are thoughts and feelings that harass us, we can test them in the same way and claim release. Christians are to be warriors, fighting with the power of the cross. "They have conquered him by the blood of the Lamb and by the word of their testimony, for they loved not their lives even unto death" (Rev. 12:11). When the devil dangles confessed sins before our eyes and tells us that we are not forgiven, we must remind him of the truth of 1 John 1:9, "If we confess our sins, he is faithful and just, and will forgive our sins and cleanse us from all unrighteousness." Through faith the believer can thank God that he is forgiven, even when he does not feel forgiven.

Fighting, we shall be victorious
By the Blood of Christ our Lord;
On our foreheads, bright and glorious,
Shines the witness of his word;
"Victory!" our song shall be
Like the thunder of the sea.

Justus Falckner, 1672-1723
Tr. Emma Frances Bevan, 1827-1909

VIII. SONGS OF VICTORY AWAIT THE FAITHFUL

(Revelation 14-16)

Judgment began when the seals were opened; more severe judgments followed as the trumpets were blown. Now the final and complete series of judgments, the bowls of wrath, are about to be poured out. In the last lesson (Revelation 12 and 13) we saw the reason for all the persecution and harassment of the Christians. It was Satan's hatred for Christ. When he was not able to hinder Jesus' great work of redemption, he attacked the followers of the Lamb, causing many of them to be martyred.

According to the closing chapters of the Revelation, the doom of the dragon, the beast, and the false prophet is sure. The bowls of wrath will be poured out on the headquarters of the beast and on all who follow him. It will be a trying time for Christians, and many will be tempted to deny the faith in order to escape persecution. But again, in his tender mercy, God gives John another picture of all the redeemed who have come through persecution victoriously. Like triumphant warriors they stand with their leader, the Lamb, on the heavenly Mount Zion, singing a new song, the song of Moses and the Lamb.

Recall that before both the seals and the trumpet judgments, Jesus gave to John beautiful visions of the redeemed in heaven, to strengthen persecuted Christians and to give them hope and courage to endure. Through all these glorious visions of heaven the Lord is saying to his people, "Be faithful to me. Do not deny me, whatever the cost. And soon you will be with me singing the triumphant songs of those who have conquered."

THE NEW SONG (Rev. 14:1-5)

Note the contrast between these chapters and the preceding ones.

Here we see the holy angels and the Lamb surrounded by his joyous followers. In Revelation 12 and 13 we saw the three unholy ones, the dragon and the two beasts.

Here we see the mark which identifies those who belong to the Lamb. There we saw the mark of the beast.

Here is beauty, joy, glory, triumph, singing, music, majesty. In the preceding chapters were fear, deceit, hatred, blasphemy, men worshiping the dragon rather than the Lamb, persecution of the saints, and satanic signs and activity.

In Revelation 12 and 13 we were looking from the earthly perspective. In Revelation 14 and 15 we are looking from the heavenly perspective.

In the Old Testament, *Zion* referred to the city of God, the earthly Jerusalem. Here it refers to the new Jerusalem, heaven itself, and points forward to the final victory which is coming to the saints when all of history will have found its consummation in Christ.

The redeemed have the name of Jesus and the Father on their foreheads. He is their love, their joy, their thought, their all. And he loves them with an everlasting love. He has been with them through every trial and now they are at home with him, safe and victorious in the Father's house. Every one of them is there. The 144,000 refers to the sum total of all the redeemed. We do not know how many that is, but God knows. He knows the name of every one of his redeemed; not one of his own will be missing.

The song they sing is a unique song for it can be sung only by forgiven sinners. Whoever has learned to sing the song of salvation has discovered a new thing; in Christ, the old has passed away and all things have become new. These redeemed ones learned to sing the new song while on earth. They chose to renounce their sins, to follow Christ, and to be loyal to him.

There are some commentators who interpret Revelation 14:4 literally, saying that this verse refers to a select group of believers who have refrained from marriage. In the Old Testament, however, any idolatry or identification with the heathen world was spoken of as "spiritual fornication." The Bible has never pronounced a special blessing on those who live a celibate life, nor has it condemned marriage. Perhaps the best commentary on this verse is the last part of verse 4, "they follow the Lamb wherever he goes." They have remained loyal to him, refusing to be seduced by the enticements of the world or to be deceived by the lies of the devil. The path of the Lamb led to the cross; so these have denied themselves, taken up their cross, and followed him, some even unto death. But now they are standing before him spotless, rejoicing in his presence.

THE MESSAGE OF THE THREE ANGELS (Rev. 14:6-11)

The first angel (Rev. 14:6-7) comes with the changeless, eternal gospel, pleading with godless men to make use of this last opportunity to repent. He flies in midheaven so that everyone will hear. He pleads with them to turn from the worship of their false gods, whatever they may be. He calls them to worship the only true God, the God of creation who is above all and over all. He would remind them that even in judgment God is merciful, for the purpose of the judgments is to call men to repentance.

The second angel (Rev. 14:8) pronounces doom on that great seducer of the nations, Babylon. So certain is her fall that the angel speaks as if it has already taken place. The judgment on Babylon will be discussed fully in Revelation 17 and 18.

The third angel (Rev. 14:9-11) enforces the message of the first angel. God is a God of love and mercy and would not have anyone be lost. He sends forth his gospel to all the world to let men know that he loves them, that he has died for them, and wants them all with him in the heavenly home. But if they refuse his love, persisting in going their own way, worshiping their own god and clinging to the enticements of the world, God must let them have their own way. One of the aspects of the wrath of God is that God turns men over to themselves and their sin when they reject God's offer of salvation. Thus man makes judgment inevitable.

The eternal agony and suffering of the lost is described in Rev. 14: 10-11. The words, "in the presence of the holy angels and in the presence of the Lamb," seems to indicate that the suffering of the lost will be intensified by an awareness of what they have forfeited. What agony it will be for those who have rejected Christ and have died without responding to his love, to look back over their lives and to realize that it could have been different—to contemplate opportunities they had to yield to Christ, now lost forever. But that which will cause the greatest pain of all will be the awareness of the blessedness of heaven, to see the angels and the Lamb, the joy and the victory, and to realize that they are eternally shut out from these blessings which could have been theirs.

Can we read these tragic words without weeping for those who reject Christ? Should not these words send us out onto the highways of life with the gracious invitation of the gospel to encourage people to accept Life?

COURAGE AND HOPE FOR CHRISTIANS (Rev. 14:12-13)

The doom of those who reject Christ, persecute Christians, and follow the beast should encourage followers of the Lamb to remain faithful to him even though it may mean persecution or death. And should this happen, let them remember the beautiful pictures of heaven with the victorious saints rejoicing in the very presence of Jesus. Let them know that God will remember their faithfulness, their labors even to the point of weariness, and their persecutions. All work done because of their love for Jesus will follow them into eternity.

HARVEST TIME (Rev. 14:14-20)

In the gospels Jesus spoke on several occasions about the end of the age when he would come to separate the chaff from the grain, the sheep from the goats, to gather his elect from the ends of the earth. The final judgment is certain. This passage in Revelation 14 gives us a preview of this judgment; it will be described more fully in later chapters. The one sitting on a white cloud wearing a golden crown, and wielding a sharp sickle in his hand is the victorious Christ. Some commentators feel that verses 14-16 refer to the harvest or gathering of Christians. The second paragraph, Revelation 14:17-20 is said to refer to the judgment on the wicked. Another interpretation holds that Revelation 14:14-16 refers to the general judgment which would include both the righteous and the wicked; vv. 17-20 would refer more specifically to the judgment on the unrighteous. Note that it is when the grapes are fully ripe that the harvest takes place. This indicates that God is in control of history which is moving steadily toward its end. When the world is ripe for judgment—only God knows the time—the Messiah will come to execute that judgment. History is not moving along meaninglessly or without direction as it so often seems. Some day he will end history so that he can bring in a new order.

THE SONG OF MOSES AND THE LAMB (Revelation 15)

We are approaching the final series of judgments, the bowls of wrath. Seven angels stand poised ready to pour out the seven last plagues. Before this happens, the suffering saints, many of whom will be martyred, are permitted to look into heaven. There they see the company of those who have conquered the beast and have refused every temptation to compromise the truth. They have stood firmly against any edict to worship the state; they have not been taken in by the lamb-like speech of the false prophet. They have followed the Lamb even to death, being martyred for their loyalty to Jesus. Now they are standing beside the sea of glass singing songs of joy to the One who has redeemed them and brought them safely through to victory. Their martyrdom, which seemed to be a victory for the beast, was in truth his defeat—but their triumph.

Their triumph reminds us of another such triumph in the Old Testament. The children of Israel were rescued from their beast, the Pharaoh, and were led safely and miraculously through the Red Sea. Standing on the shores of that sea, they too, sang a song of triumph (Exod. 15:1-18).

The martyrs sing, not only the song of Moses, but also the song of the Lamb. This is the song of redemption, the song of the pioneer of their faith who went before them to death and who through that death, opened for them the way to glory. As Moses delivered the Israelites from Pharaoh, so Jesus will deliver his people out of the hands of the beast.

This song of the victorious Christians is a song of anticipation. It will be sung in the future after the final consummation. As the persecuted Christians see the joyous company of martyrs and hear their songs of triumph they can project themselves into the picture and know that if they continue to follow the Lamb, even to martyrdom, they, too will someday be a part of that victorious band.

The seven angels who execute the final judgments are now described (Rev. 15:5-8). They come from the very presence of God and are dressed in glorious apparel. They hold golden bowls which are filled with the wrath of God. This whole scene tells us that the wrath of God is his holiness reacting against sin. God had called to men through the seals and the trumpet judgments but they had refused to repent. They had rejected God's offer of love in Christ. Now their cup of iniquity is full, and instead of experiencing God's love, they will experience his wrath.

THE SEVEN BOWLS OF WRATH (Revelation 16)

At the direct command of God the seven angels pour out the wrath of God upon the earth. These judgments are very similar to the trumpet judgments (Rev. 8-9) and both bear a resemblance to the plagues of Egypt.

The *first bowl of wrath* is directed against men who wear the mark of the beast. This affliction is like the boils which came upon the Egyptians. It is unlike the first four trumpet judgments for they did not touch the person but were directed against nature.

The *second bowl* turns the sea into blood. This is similar to the second trumpet but with this difference—the second trumpet judgment affected only one-third of the sea. Here the whole sea becomes blood.

The *third bowl* causes the rivers and fountains of water to turn to blood. Similarly, the third trumpet caused a star called Wormwood to fall into the rivers and fountains of waters which made one-third of them bitter and poisonous. As a result many people died. The third bowl turns all the waters into blood. Because of this, it would seem that more people died from this plague than from the results of the third trumpet.

The beast through his henchmen and followers had caused much blood to flow in the martyrdom of the many followers of the Lamb. Now they are given blood to drink. The angel of the waters proclaims that God's judgment here is just. The altar (which is personified) answers (Rev. 16:7), agreeing that God is righteous and just in sending this plague. The altar may refer to the prayers of the saints or to the cries of the martyrs (Rev. 6:9) that God would avenge his persecuted and martyred children. These prayers are now being answered in the pouring out of the bowls of wrath; the martyred saints have not been forgotten by God. His judgments are true and just. God is vindicated in his judgments.

The *fourth bowl* affects the sun as did the fourth trumpet. But again, the trumpet judgment was partial, darkening one-third of the sun, moon, and stars. This plague is more severe, for it causes intense pain. Note that the sun *was allowed* to scorch men, indicating that God was permitting this painful plague. The men who are scorched realize the hand of God in this, for they curse him rather than repent and acknowledge the glory and sovereignty of God.

The *fifth bowl* is directed at the throne or headquarters of the beast, which could refer to Rome as the center of the anti-Christian government in John's day, or it could refer to the world dominion of antichrist. The plague of darkness intensifies the pain caused by the other plagues. But again, evil men refuse to repent. They curse God, gnawing their tongues in anguish.

The *sixth bowl* is different from the others in that it does not cause any pain to the enemies of God. Rather it dries up the Euphrates River so that the kings of the East may pass over it. The Euphrates formed the boundary between Israel and her heathen enemies. The removal of this barrier is symbolically portrayed in the drying up of the river. There are several instances in Scripture, the Red Sea episode being one example, where the drying of a river indicated the power of God.

The unholy trinity—the dragon (the devil), the beast (the anti-Christian political and military systems) and the false prophet (anti-Christian religious systems)—angered because of the pain and judgments inflicted on them, now determine to make a final war on the Messiah and his followers. Through the means of demonic power, symbolized by the frogs, they influence the kings of the whole godless civilization, to join forces with the pagan hordes to make war on Christ and his followers. Their strategy and plans are inspired by hell itself. This bowl calls to mind the sixth trumpet where a demonic horde killed a third of mankind.

Because this final battle will be such a great test for the Christian and because it will occur suddenly, John interjects, in the name of the Lord, a warning and an encouragement (Rev. 16:15). Just when the battle will be at its height and it would seem that the cause of the Messiah and his people is being lost, at that moment Christ will appear to deliver his own and to defeat every enemy. Therefore Christians are to keep their eyes on him, loving, waiting for, and hastening his appearing. They are not to be taken by surprise knowing that he will come unexpectedly like a thief (Rev. 16:15). They will not sleep but will keep alert for signs of his coming. They will live each day in his presence, motivated to holy living by the thought, "Perhaps he will come today!"

Armageddon is a term which not only the Christian, but also the secular world, associates with the final holocaust which will end history. Most scholars hold that Armageddon is a compound of two Hebrew words, one meaning *mountain* and the other *Megiddo,* the name of a broad valley where God came to the rescue of his people in many decisive battles; thus the term Mount Megiddo, or Armageddon is said to refer to this large plain where God fought for his people.

Many interpretations have been given to the battle of *Armageddon.* Those who interpret Armageddon literally believe that it refers to an actual battle which will take place on the plain of Esdraelon near Megiddo in the holy land. They believe that in this final battle the enemies of Christ under the leadership of antichrist will make war on the Christian forces. At a decisive moment Christ will appear to defeat antichrist and to save his own.

Another view holds that Armageddon does not refer to a geographical location nor to an armed battle, but to the final struggle between Christ and Satan. When the conflict becomes the fiercest, Christ will appear suddenly to rescue his people and to defeat every enemy.

The seventh bowl is the climax of the series of judgments; it describes the collapse of Babylon, symbolizing the center of anti-Christian world power. To the early Christian this would refer to Rome which was the headquarters for the beast (Domitian, the Roman governor). But eschatologically it refers to "the sum total of pagan culture, social, intellectual, and commercial that had opposed and oppressed the people of God from time immemorial." (Tenney)

The seventh bowl is poured into the air, implying that life on earth will cease. The great voice which calls from out of the temple is God himself proclaiming from his throne in heaven that the judgments are now completed and that the end of this world has come. All the cataclysmic occurrences in nature symbolize the power, holiness, and glory of God. His wrath, which is his holiness reacting against sin, is poured out on Babylon, the capital of the beast. An earthquake breaks it into three pieces, symbolizing the complete disintegration and collapse of non-Christian culture and civilization.

God remembered Babylon (Rev. 16:19). It was she who had persecuted and killed the followers of the Lamb. God was aware of all their sufferings; he had heard their cries and prayers that his honor would be avenged; he had not forgotten them. Now the time had come. The followers of the beast had seen the hand of God in the seal and trumpet judgments, but they had refused to repent. Now they must drain the cup of the fury of God's wrath. Convulsions in nature, including hail stones which weighed over 60 pounds each, did not evoke any kind of repentance. Instead the enemies of God cursed him even though they realized that history was at an end.

The statement, "Every island fled away" (Rev. 16:21), perhaps looks ahead to the complete renovation and restoration of this world when everything in this created order will become new.

Note that the bowls of wrath are poured out on the beast, his followers, and on his throne. God's children may experience suffering, persecution, and martyrdom, but they will never experience God's wrath. That is reserved for his enemies.

The message to the world is this: history is moving steadily and surely toward its close. God is in perfect control. He calls men to repentance through every means possible. He sends out his gospel to the whole earth. But when men refuse to acknowledge God, spurn his love and continue in their sins, then God, after much patience and longsuffering must let man have his own way. Scripture states that unrepentant man will experience God's wrath.

"He who believes in the Son has eternal life; he who does not obey the Son shall not see life, but the wrath of God rests upon him" (John 3:36).

The message for the Christian is this: In Christ your victory is certain. The devil may harass you; suffering and persecution may plague you; martyrdom may be your lot. But God has not forgotten you; he knows your every trial; he is aware of every pain and tear. He is working on your behalf because you are very precious to him. So follow the Lamb and be loyal to him. Refuse any temptation to compromise. Be alert to the deceptions of the enemy. Keep looking for the return of your Lord. And some day you will join that joyous, victorious multitude, singing the song of Moses and the Lamb.

Am I a soldier of the Cross,
A follower of the Lamb,
And shall I fear to own his cause
Or blush to speak his Name?

Sure I must fight, if I would reign—
Increase my courage, Lord—
I'll bear the toil, endure the pain,
Supported by thy word.

Thy saints, in all this glorious war,
Shall conquer, though they die;
They see the triumph from afar,
By faith they bring it nigh.

When that illustrious day shall rise,
And all thy armies shine
In robes of victory through the skies,
The glory shall be thine.

Isaac Watts, 1674-1748.

IX. ONLY TREASURES ROOTED IN CHRIST WILL LAST

(Revelation 17 and 18)

As the book of Revelation moves toward its close, we see history also moving toward its close. The final series of judgments, the bowls of wrath, have been poured out on the beast and his followers. After the final bowl of wrath was emptied, the voice of God was heard saying, "It is done!" Judgment on the earth is now completed. All that remains is to dispose of the enemies. The dragon, the beast, the false prophet, Babylon and death—which is the last enemy—will all be destroyed. Their destruction is described in Revelation 17-20. Their removal makes way for the new heaven and earth which is the subject of Revelation 21 and 22.

The last bowl of wrath to be poured out (Rev. 16:17-21) caused the great city of Babylon to collapse. In Revelation 14:8 the fall of Babylon had been predicted. Now in Revelation 17 and 18 Babylon and her destruction are described.

THE SYMBOLIC MEANING OF BABYLON

Who is this Babylon? What does she symbolize? Let us recall the history of Babylon in the Old Testament to help us understand the symbolic meaning. The beginning of Babylon stems from the time after the flood when the people, in obvious defiance of God, built a high tower so that they could be independent of God (Gen. 11:4). Thus we see that the tower of Babel (and later Babylon) symbolized pride, defiance of God, a desire to live independently of God, and a rebellious spirit that chose sin in preference to God's laws.

To the readers of the Revelation in John's day, all that Babylon stood for in past history was now embodied in Rome. The Roman government under Domitian was the great enemy of the Christian.

THE CHARACTER AND ACTIVITY OF BABYLON THE HARLOT
(Rev. 17:1-6)

Again John is "in the Spirit" (v. 3), indicating that another vision is about to unfold before his eyes. In his vision he is carried into the wilderness where he sees the figure of a woman seated upon a beast which is emerging from the waters. The waters represent "peoples and multitudes and nations and tongues" (Rev. 17:15). The beast seems to be the same beast which was introduced in Revelation 13 representing all the governments and systems in the world which are hostile to Christianity.

The woman is called a harlot. This term was familiar to Old Testa-

65

ment readers because any idolatry, any unfaithfulness to God on the part of Israel was spoken of as spiritual adultery or harlotry. The woman is dressed like a harlot in her lavish and garish attire which is meant to attract followers. Those who are taken in by her extravagant appeal, the kings of the earth and the dwellers on earth (secular society) become drunk with her wine. She, too, is drunk with the "blood of the saints and the blood of the martyrs of Jesus" (Rev. 17:6), for she had caused the death of many of God's children.

The woman is another of the devil's allies. Like the other henchmen of Satan, she is a deceiver. Through her glamour, wealth, industry, commerce, and pagan culture she seeks to seduce and entice the nations of the world away from faith in the true God. She is the spirit of the world that is anti-Christ, anti-God.

She symbolizes the Rome of John's day which was characterized by affluence, debauchery, crime, immorality, and a hatred for Christianity which took delight in torturing Christians. However, Babylon goes beyond historical Rome. She symbolizes any non-Christian civilization or system which worships the world, hates the Christian, and seeks to seduce people away from God.

The woman has a name of mystery on her forehead. It was customary in ancient times for prostitutes to identify themselves by means of a headband. Her name identifies her as the *mother* of harlots (Rev. 17:5). Not only does she entice people away from God, but she enlists her followers to do the same. It is said that astrology was the chief religion in ancient Babylon. Thus Babylon refers to a secular civilization which wears the facade of religion. Some interpreters believe that Babylon symbolizes the false church that gets its support from anti-Christian governments. Babylon rides on the beast.

THE MYSTERY OF THE WOMAN AND THE BEAST (Rev. 17:7-18)

John is amazed at the appearance of the woman. The angel hastens to interpret the meaning of the woman and the beast. This explanation is very puzzling and difficult to understand. The beast, as stated previously, is to be identified with the beast of Revelation 13 for they both have seven heads and ten horns, representing kingdoms and nations which have followed the beast. The beast is said to have had an existence in the past, *he was;* at the present writing, *he is not;* but in the future, *he will exist again* (Rev. 17:8). This is similar to the beast of Revelation 13 who had a mortal wound which was healed.

The beast may have reminded the readers of Nero who persecuted the Christians, committed suicide, and then was rumored to have come back to life. However, the beast in Revelation 17 is said to "ascend from the bottomless pit." This means that he comes from the place of demonic spirits in the power of Satan. This passage may mean that the spirit of men like Nero, Domitian, Mao, and others who have done the devil's work in their hatred of Christians, will at the end of the age culminate in the person of antichrist who will be Satan incarnate.

Every civilization and ruler who has defied God and tried to eradicate Christianity has gone down to defeat. But they rear their heads in the form of other God-defying systems which have the same spirit of hatred for the Lamb and his followers. But they will go down to perdition once and for all. Their doom is described in Revelation 19. The angel states that the godless and those without salvation (those whose names are not in the book of life) will marvel when they see the beast revived time and time again in history (Rev. 17:8). Especially at the end of the age they will not only marvel but will pay homage and follow him, not realizing that his doom is sure.

Wisdom is needed to understand these difficult verses (Rev. 17:9-14). The seven heads of the beast are said to be seven hills on which the woman is seated. This would seem to refer to Rome, for tradition says that Rome was built on seven hills. But the heads are also seven kings (Rev. 17:10). This could refer to rulers or kingdoms which have been hostile to Christianity. Five are in the past; one, Rome, was in power when John wrote, and one is to come. This one could refer to the last world empire through which antichrist will wield his power.

"The beast that was and is not, it is an eighth but it belongs to the seven" (Rev. 17:11). This is perhaps one of the most difficult passages in the Revelation. It may mean that following a succession of rulers who are hostile to Christianity and are in reality antichrists, a final one will emerge, the eighth, who is like the others in his hatred of Christ, and yet unique and distinct from them.

Since the symbolic meaning of seven is completeness, the seven hills and the seven heads perhaps refer not only to Rome but to all the world's kingdoms and rulers who have been hostile to Christ and his kingdom. The harlot, Babylon, has always exerted her devastating influence through such kingdoms.

The 10 horn kings (Rev. 17:12) have been the subject of much discussion. They had not yet appeared on the scene when John wrote. One contemporary author believes that when 10 nations have joined the European common market, this will be a fulfillment of the reference to the 10 kings. Beckwith believes that they are "purely eschatological figures representing the totality of the powers of all nations on the earth which are to be made subservient to Antichrist." Perhaps it is wise not to speculate as to their identity.

HOPE FOR CHRISTIANS

Into the darkness of this picture John interjects a light of hope and courage for the tested and tried Christian (Rev. 17:14). The Lamb will conquer the beast and his cohorts. He is the King of kings and Lord of lords. All those who oppose him will last but an hour. None can stand before him. And all who belong to Christ will share his victory. Therefore, let the Christian continue faithful to the Lamb, for even though it may seem that the forces of Satan are winning, Christ will be the ultimate victor.

67

John now returns to the subject of the harlot (Rev. 17:15-18). In the previous paragraph most of the discussion has centered on the beast. The harlot is seated upon waters which represent "peoples and multitudes and nations and tongues," indicating the worldwide influence of the harlot. She seems to have been very successful. Through her allure, glamour, fascination, power, and religious facade, she has influenced the whole world to follow her and to make a god of materialistic values. In his first letter, John characterized her in the words, "the lust of the flesh, the lust of the eyes and the vain glory of life." Every anti-Christian government has promoted her ideology.

But now we see a surprising development. The powers that have been supporting her, the beast and the 10 horns, turn on the harlot and destroy her. One interpretation of this passage is that it is the revived Nero who comes with his Parthian cohorts and destroys Rome. But perhaps this event has more far-reaching implications than historical Rome. Godless, materialistic civilization, directed, organized, and propagated by Satan and his henchmen for one purpose, to oppose God and his kingdom, will continue only as long as God permits. It is rushing toward its destruction. In a mysterious way God seems to permit evil to destroy itself. The beast will turn on his own ally, the harlot. Is this not, in a sense, happening today in the ecology and energy crisis, in the arms race, in the lust for power and material things? Man is destroying himself and his own world. Is this not true also on the personal level? An individual who drinks of the world's wine and lives solely on the physical, materialistic level soon discovers that life has lost its meaning. Many such people end their lives in desperation. But on a broader level, this passage is saying that one day the whole God-defying, materialistic civilization will be destroyed in order to make way for God's new world where righteousness will reign.

THE DESTRUCTION OF BABYLON (Rev. 18:1-8)

The identity, character, and influence of Babylon, the harlot, was described in Revelation 17. In this chapter her destruction and the lament of her devotees are portrayed. The angel reechoes the same words of another angel in Rev. 14:8, "Fallen, fallen is Babylon the great." Again it is stated in the past tense as if it had already taken place. We must keep in mind that John is here describing the collapse of eschatological Babylon, the complete destruction of godless civilization which will take place at the end of the age. The words which the writer uses to describe the utter devastation of Babylon are taken from the prophesies of Isaiah and Jeremiah pronouncing the doom of Babylon and Nineveh. These prophecies have been literally fulfilled in relation to these cities. Babylon over the centuries has remained uninhabited (Rev. 18:2).

The cause of her destruction is now given (Rev. 18:3). Her one driving aim has been to draw people away from worship of the true God to the worship of the beast. To do this she has used the seductive powers of a harlot and the glamour and wealth of a city. The nations of the world and the merchants of the earth believed her lies, drank her wine, and became infatuated with her riches and pleasures.

A voice of warning is sounded (Rev. 18:4-5). God's people are called upon to separate themselves from Babylon because if they identify with her they will also experience her plagues. Because of the severe persecution and the resultant martyrdom of many followers of the Lamb, many Christians might be tempted to affiliate with Babylon in order to escape. But the warning here is to remember the certain doom of Babylon and all her followers. God's call to his people has always been to come out and to be separate from the world.

The justice of God's judgment on Babylon is now related (Rev. 18:6-8). Babylon has defied God, martyred the saints, and has tricked the world into believing that it could get along very well without God. She has lived in self-indulgence, luxury, and pride, boasting, "A queen I sit, I am no widow, mourning I shall never see." But God has not forgotten her sins nor her treatment of his beloved children. The deification of herself has been accumulating the wrath of God and now suddenly, in a single hour, she will be brought down from her arrogant perch and completely devastated. She has caused the Christians great suffering. Now she will be repaid in double measure. Plagues, pestilence, mourning, and famine will ruin her. Her doom is certain because God is just. "Whatsoever a man sows that shall he also reap." God is mighty; he is able to bring Babylon to utter ruin.

THE LAMENT OF BABYLON'S DEVOTEES (Rev. 18:9-19)

The kings of the earth are the first who lament the ruin of Babylon (Rev. 18:9-10). They had been taken in by her lies, believing that worldly power, materialistic success, and technological advances would guarantee their own security and success. Now as they see the object of their affections going up in smoke, they realize it was all a lie. They have been duped. Standing at a distance, terrified by her torment, they utter their doleful dirge, "Alas! alas! thou great city, thou mighty city, Babylon."

The merchants of the earth are the next to join the chorus of dirges (Rev. 18:11-17). They weep and mourn because their business has failed. The bottom has dropped out. Their grief is entirely selfish; they weep not so much for the city itself as for what its destruction has done to them economically.

The list of items which make up the cargo speak of the luxury and extravagance of the wares which found their way from distant places to the ports of Rome. There were precious stones from India, silk from China (it was said that silk was so expensive that a pound cost a pound of gold), sweet smelling spices from Arabia, wood and ivory from Africa, and slaves from any country that would supply them (Rev. 18:13).

The opulent, self-indulgent way of life that characterized ancient Rome is well documented by historians. Her destruction prefigures the eschatological destruction of the great city, Babylon. All the merchants of the earth, all people who have invested heavily in the cargoes of this world, forgetting that the only lasting treasures are the heavenly ones, will one day realize their folly. There was nothing intrinsically wrong with these wares. All of them are beautiful gifts of God meant to enhance life and to bring joy to man. But Babylon used them to entice men away from God. And mankind succumbed to her wiles, making the wares themselves their god.

What tragedy! The godless had looked to material success to satisfy them and to give them the good life. Now they realize that it has all evaporated; the splendors of Babylon are lost forever (Rev. 18:14). Like the kings of the earth, the merchants also stand far off, watching sadly as Babylon falls to her ruin, but not lifting a finger to help. They had no real love for Babylon; it was the wealth which Babylon had brought to the merchants which bound them to her. In their lament (Rev. 18: 15-17a) they admit that all the glamour, beauty, and wealth which characterized Babylon, the harlot, was but a facade. There was nothing there of eternal value. Now they are left bankrupt; that on which they had pinned their hopes is gone forever.

Next the shipmasters, seafaring men, and sailors raise their voices and join the lament (Rev. 18:17b-19). In Oriental fashion they show their grief by throwing dust on their heads. Like the merchants, their sorrow is purely selfish. They cry not for the city itself, but because now that she lies in ruins, the ship owners will no longer grow rich from her wealth.

A CAUSE FOR REJOICING (Rev. 18:20)

Into the series of doleful laments is interjected a note of triumphant praise. The saints, apostles, and prophets are called on to praise God; for now all the outrages against Christ and his people have been avenged. Babylon the great, the enemy of God and the persecuter of his people, has been destroyed. Now God can bring in the new heaven and the new earth peopled by a society made new in Christ.

THE FINAL LAMENT OVER BABYLON (Rev. 18:21-24)

The previous laments were uttered by the business and commercial interests in the world. This lament is pronounced by an angel. The complete and final destruction of the God-defying world system is now symbolized by the angel as he hurls a huge millstone into the depths of the sea from which it can never rise. In similar fashion, Jeremiah was commanded to write on a scroll the prophesy of the destruction of historical Babylon and hurl it into the Euphrates (Jer. 51:63-64).

There is sadness and tragedy in that haunting refrain, "No more" repeated six times. It is as though the angel is contemplating what could have been—what glory could have belonged to Babylon, had she not turned from God and used all her powers to seduce others away from him. There seems to be an ascending climax in the use of the words, "no more." No more music, no more craftsmen, none to grind wheat to sustain life, no more light—utter darkness, no more love or the joys of family life. All the things mentioned could have enhanced and beautified life. But now they are all stripped away and those who have followed Babylon are left bereft, bankrupt, eternally desolate. Again the reason for Babylon's destruction is given. She had promoted wealthy tycoons who were full of arrogance and pride; she had seduced the nations of the world into thinking they could manage without God and that living on the materialistic level meant happiness and success; and finally she was responsible for the martyrdom of countless of God's faithful followers, not only in Rome, but all over the earth (Rev. 18:23b-24).

BABYLON TODAY

As we contemplate John's descriptions of Babylon, we are struck by the many similarities to our world today. We conclude that Babylon is still with us and will be until she is finally destroyed at the second advent of Christ.

What are some marks of contemporary Babylon?

1. *Between the nations of the world:* the arms race, distrust among nations, lust for power, war, planning and seeking peace without God, depending on technology for security rather than on God.

2. *Within society:* lust for things, pleasure-madness, crime, corruption, permissiveness, hard core pornography. Historian and columnist Max Lerner says, "We're living in a Babylonian society, perhaps more Babylonian than Babylon itself."

3. *In religion and the church:* the growing interest in the occult and Eastern religions which are attracting thousands of people; false religions which deny the deity and vicarious atonement of Jesus Christ; the tendency in some Christian groups to emphasize social action and community outreach to the exclusion of the preaching of the gospel; the tendency in other groups to become so ingrown and concerned with their own survival that they are blinded to the needs of others; the temptation of the church to imitate and adopt the methods of the world to achieve success rather than to rely on the power of the Holy Spirit.

4. *On the personal level:* becoming too enamored with the world, permitting *things* to play too important a role in our lives, being infected with the thinking and philosophy of the world, compromising with truth and ethical behavior in order to succeed, planning without God, pride, self-sufficiency.

All are marks of Babylon.

HOW SHALL A CHRISTIAN LIVE IN A BABYLONIAN SOCIETY?

Jesus said that we are to be *in* the world but not *of* it. "If any one loves the world, love for the Father is not in him" (1 John 2:15). The call to each of us in Revelation 18:4 is to come out of Babylon and have no part in her sins. We are to be salt and light that will permeate society. We are to work for the redemption of society. And we must constantly be on our guard lest we be seduced by her glamour, remembering that her days are numbered. The whole godless world will collapse some day. So let us lay up for ourselves treasures in heaven, remembering that only what is done for Christ will have eternal significance.

O Jesus, I have promised
To serve thee to the end;
Be thou forever near me,
My master and my friend;
I shall not fear the battle
If thou art by my side,
Nor wander from the pathway
If thou wilt be my guide.

O let me feel thee near me,
The world is ever near;
I see the sights that dazzle,
The tempting sounds I hear;
My foes are ever near me,
Around me and within;
But, Jesus, draw thou nearer,
And shield my soul from sin.

John Ernest Bode 1816-74

X. CHRIST IS KING OF KINGS AND LORD OF LORDS

(Revelation 19 and 20)

Before God can usher in the new heaven and the new earth he must make way for it by eliminating every enemy and all who refuse to have a part in his kingdom. In the last lesson we witnessed the downfall of Babylon and heard the laments of those who had put all their trust in godless, materialistic values. They wail and mourn because the collapse of Babylon has left them destitute and bankrupt. In contrast to these dirges, in Revelation 19 we hear the hallelujahs of the celebration in heaven because Babylon, the great enemy of God's people has been destroyed. Revelation 19 and 20 move toward the climax of the book as every enemy is defeated.

THE HALLELUJAH CHORUS (Rev. 19:1-8)

All of heaven breaks forth into this mighty song of praise to God because he has demolished Babylon and set his people free from her tyranny. Four times we hear the word, "hallelujah," a Hebrew word meaning, "praise ye Jehovah." This word is used often in Old Testament songs of praise, especially in the Psalms. This is the only place that "hallelujah" is used in the New Testament.

John emphasizes truths through the use of contrast. The purpose is to bring courage and hope in the midst of trials. Following scenes of gloom and doom he presents visions of glory and victory. He does this here. In Revelation 18 is the harlot; in Revelation 19, the bride. In Revelation 18 there is sin, sorrow, corruption, moaning, doom, and death—all viewed from the perspective of the earth. In Revelation 19 there is righteousness, joy, purity, singing, victory, and life—all viewed from the perspective of heaven.

The first group to take up the song is *a great multitude in heaven* (Rev. 19:1), perhaps the angels. They are filled with ecstasy as they shout out their hallelujahs, praising God for this great thing which he has done. They give God all the glory for it is his work alone which has brought salvation, the complete deliverance of his people. To him belong power and , glory. The angels rejoice that the great worldly seducer, Babylon, is now out of the way. It was she who with her glamour and dazzle enticed people away from God. It was she who deceived people into making a god of this world, leading them to worship the beast. It was Babylon the harlot who caused the suffering and death of countless Christians. Now she is no more. The prayers of the saints and martyrs have been answered. No more can she harass and harm God's dear children. She has gone up in smoke, destroyed forever.

The 24 elders and the four living creatures (Rev. 19:4) now join the victory song with their "hallelujah," adding the *amen* to the song of the angels.

A voice from the throne (Rev. 19:5), perhaps one of the cherubim, exhorts everyone on earth to praise God for this great victory.

Now the whole company of heaven bursts into song (Rev. 19:6). "Hallelujah! Praise the Lord!" they exult, for now God has taken over complete control and will assert his power to bring to consummation the intended purpose for his creation. Now that Babylon is out of the way, the marriage supper of the Lamb can take place. The Old Testament writers often referred to Israel as the wife of Jehovah. Jesus, too, referred to the marriage supper; and Paul spoke of the church as being the bride of Christ.

THE MARRIAGE SUPPER OF THE LAMB (Rev. 19:7-10)

This is the event for which the church is longing and waiting. It refers to the union of Christ with his bride, the church, when he comes again. In the present time the church is united with him through faith. She has been given her wedding dress, which is the righteousness of Christ. Now as she waits for him to come and claim her she continues to prepare herself for this great event with a life of service, loyalty, love, and devotion (Rev. 19:8).

When he comes, the Bridegroom and his bride, the church, will be united forever in the new heaven and the new earth.

Small wonder that the whole company of heaven, the Old and New Testament saints and martyrs and every child of God on earth, are called upon to join in this great hallelujah chorus. Handel has echoed the victory and triumph of this scene beautifully in the "Hallelujah Chorus" in his *Messiah.*

The angel now pronounces a blessing on those who are invited to this marriage supper (Rev. 19:9). This includes not only the invitation but also the response. Only those who respond to the invitation by acknowledging their sin and need, by accepting the wedding garment of forgiveness and Christ's righteousness, and who keep the oil of the Holy Spirit in their lives, will have the privilege of participating in the great marriage supper of the Lamb. What a joy it will be to have fellowship with Abraham, Isaac, Jacob, and all the other Old Testament heroes of faith; with Matthew, Mark, Luke, John, Paul, and scores of New Testament saints and martyrs! John is so overwhelmed at the prospect of this joyous gathering that he falls prostrate before the angel. Perhaps he thinks the voice he hears is that of Christ or God. However, the angel puts himself on the same level as John and other Christians in the matter of worship. He states emphatically that God is the only one who is to be worshiped.

CHRIST RETURNS—THE KING OF KINGS AND THE LORD OF LORDS (Rev. 19:11-16)

At last the climactic moment in history has arrived; Christ comes again to defeat every foe and to bring to fruition the kingdom of God on earth.

In the previous paragraph (Rev. 19:9-10) the marriage supper of the Lamb was promised but was not actually described; but here is the fulfillment of the union of the heavenly Bridegroom with his bride, the church.

Up until this point in the Revelation it has seemed as though the enemies of God were in control; the seals, the trumpets, and the bowls of wrath have brought disaster and destruction upon the earth. The beast was permitted to make war on the saints and to conquer them (Rev. 13:7). Countless Christians have been persecuted and martyred. But God has been in control all along. These enemies exist only as long as God permits it. But at last he openly asserts his control and from now on in the Revelation we see him defeating every remaining enemy to make way for the new heaven and the new earth.

As heaven is opened John is given a vision of the returning, conquering Christ. In Revelation 4 a door was opened into heaven and John saw God on the throne and Jesus, the Lamb, holding the scroll of destiny. The contents of the scroll have now taken place and God's redemptive purposes in history have been fulfilled. Now Christ can come and consummate all of history in himself.

He comes as a warrior, riding on a white horse, white symbolizing victory. We saw another rider on a white horse in Revelation 6. That horseman also rode forth as a warrior, but it was to conquer the minds of men through deceit and evil; that rider was associated with war, famine, and death. There can be no doubt as to the identity of this rider. The titles which are ascribed to him, his appearance, and his actions all tell us that this is Christ himself, returning in power and victory.

He is called *faithful and true.* He is absolutely dependable and trustworthy. Confidently we can stake our lives and our eternal destiny on him. Every word he speaks is the truth. In him we meet ultimate reality. What a contrast with the beast who leads all who follow him to eternal destruction.

He has *eyes like a flame of fire,* looking into the innermost heart, evaluating attitudes and motivations.

He comes as the *King wearing many royal crowns.* Jesus is the King now, but it is not evident to the world. When he returns in glorious splendor, the whole world will know that he is King of kings and Lord of lords. And those who have followed the beast will realize that the crowns of the beast were but cheap counterfeits.

The name of Jesus is one which no one knows but himself (Rev. 19:12). There are hidden mysteries in the person of Christ which the human mind cannot fathom. He is called faithful and true. In a measure we can understand that. He is also called the Word of God (Rev. 19:13). John used this same term, Word or *Logos* in his gospel. It means that Jesus reveals and expresses perfectly the innermost character and message of God.

Jesus' garments are dipped in blood (Rev. 19:13). This is not the blood of the cross but the blood of his enemies. It symbolizes the triumph of Christ in the final battle with antichrist.

75

As he rides forth he is accompanied by an army of heavenly beings (Rev. 19:14), dressed in white and riding white horses. Some interpreters believe that this army represents the saints and martyrs in heaven. Others believe that they are the angels. Jesus spoke of the angels accompanying him when he returned: ". . . when he comes in the glory of his Father with the holy angels" (Mark 8:38).

However, this army does not seem to be equipped for battle. It is Jesus alone who fights this battle. With the sword of his mouth, which is the Word of God, he smites the nations (Rev. 19:15). This Word is not the gospel, but a terrible word of judgment.

As God brought the world into being with the Word, he now brings history to a close with that same powerful Word. This is the only weapon Christ uses. With the Word he brings to an end the hell which men have made of his world. In describing this, John makes use of Psalm 2 which vividly portrays the power of the Messianic king, "You shall break them with a rod of iron, and dash them in pieces like a potter's vessel."

The second coming of Christ will be a terrible and fearful thing for those who have rejected him and have followed Babylon and worshiped the beast. The first coming of Christ holds no fear for the unbelieving world; gladly they join in celebrating the birth of the lovely Child in the manger. But there will be no celebration for the world at Christ's second coming. When he rides forth triumphantly to cleanse his world in preparation for the new world, all will know unmistakably that he is King of kings and Lord of lords. Then "every knee should bow, in heaven and on earth and under the earth, and every tongue confess that Jesus Christ is Lord, to the glory of God the Father" (Phil. 2:10-11).

THE DEFEAT OF THE BEAST AND THE FALSE PROPHET
(Rev. 19:17-21)

Even before the great battle between Christ and antichrist begins, an angel, standing in the sun where he can be seen by all the birds of prey, invites the vultures to feast on the flesh of all those who have rejected Christ. What a contrast there is between this supper of God and the marriage supper of the Lamb! The marriage supper brings visions of rejoicing, victory, fellowship, and love in the presence of the Bridegroom throughout all eternity. But the supper of God described here brings utter tragedy, despair, alienation, and hopelessness forever.

The participants in the battle now assemble. The beast and the kings of the earth, symbolizing the anti-Christian political and military world system headed by antichrist, gather their forces to make war on the Messiah. The battle itself is not described. The emphasis is on the decisive victory of Christ over antichrist. The beast and the false prophet are both captured and thrown alive into the lake of fire. These are the two beasts of Revelation 13. The false prophet represents the priestly system which enforced emperor worship during the reign of Domitian. In a broader sense he represents all religions and philosophies which deny and reject the person and work of Christ. When Christ comes again every religious and political system, every nation, every individual that refuses to bow before Christ and acknowledge him as Savior and Lord will be given what has been chosen—separation from God forever.

EVERY ENEMY DEFEATED AT LAST (Revelation 20)

Before looking into the meaning of the details in this chapter, let us summarize the events as they are presented.

First, Satan is bound for a thousand years (Rev. 20:1-3). At the beginning of this period, the saints and martyrs are resurrected and reign with Christ during this thousand year period (Rev. 20:4-6). At the end of this period Satan is set free and the enemies of God make war on Christ and his saints. Christ defeats them and Satan is thrown into the lake of fire where the beast and the false prophet have also been thrown (Rev. 20:7-10). Finally we see the great white throne where every individual will be judged and his final destiny sealed. Death and Hades are thrown into the lake of fire along with those whose names are not written in the Lamb's book of life (Rev. 20:11-15). Everything is now ready for the new heaven and the new earth.

THE MILLENNIUM

The literal meaning of the word *millennium* is a period of a thousand years and here it refers to the thousand year reign of Christ as stated in Revelation 20. This is the only place in the Bible where *millennium* is used, yet it has become a subject of great interest and controversy. We will look at three interpretations of the millennium.

The Postmillennial View holds that the millennium does not refer to a literal thousand years, but symbolizes the whole age from the coming of Christ to his coming again. During this time the church will grow and Christianity will have such a great influence on the world that most people will become Christians. Evil will be subdued (the devil bound), righteousness will triumph, and the golden age of the kingdom of God will be ushered in. Then Christ will come. Christ comes *after* the symbolic millennium; hence the term *postmillennialism*.

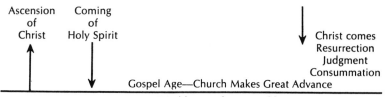

Ascension of Christ

Coming of Holy Spirit

Christ comes
Resurrection
Judgment
Consummation

Gospel Age—Church Makes Great Advance

World grows better and better.

Postmillennial View

The Premillennial View says that Christ will come *before* the thousand year period and reign a thousand years on earth. The thousand years may be taken literally or may refer to an ideal time, long or short.

Premillennialists believe that the Revelation describes a chronological series of events relating to the second coming of Christ which should be interpreted as literally as possible. The first event is the "rapture" of the church (a Greek word meaning "to be caught up").

According to this view the marriage supper of the Lamb follows (Rev. 19:7-9). While the glorified church is rejoicing with Christ in heaven, the Great Tribulation takes place on earth under the reign of the Antichrist. Following this period of suffering, Christ comes again, this time with his saints. Satan is bound for a thousand years, his power curbed so that he cannot deceive the nations. Christ reigns on earth for a thousand years and enforces righteousness. At the end of this period, Satan is set free to deceive the nations again and to gather all the enemies of God to battle against Christ and his people. But Christ defeats the enemy and the devil is thrown into the lake of fire where the beast and the false prophet have already been thrown.

Then follows the resurrection of the unbelieving dead. The premillennial view holds to two resurrections, the resurrection of believers before the thousand year period and the resurrection of the unsaved after the millennium is over. After the judgment at the great white throne the new heaven and the new earth are ushered in. There is not complete agreement among premillennialists as to the order of events. The following chart represents a view held quite generally.

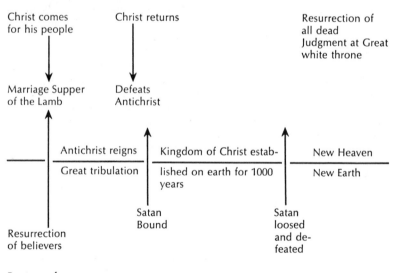

Christ comes for his people

Christ returns

Resurrection of all dead
Judgment at Great white throne

Marriage Supper of the Lamb

Defeats Antichrist

Antichrist reigns

Great tribulation

Kingdom of Christ established on earth for 1000 years

New Heaven

New Earth

Satan Bound

Satan loosed and defeated

Resurrection of believers

Rapture of the church

The amillennial view holds that there is no literal millennium but that the thousand years symbolize the entire church age. This view denies that the thousand years means that during the church age there is to be either a period of righteousness and peace, as set forth by postmillennialism, or a personal, visible reign of Christ *on earth* with the saints, as set forth by premillennialism. Amillennialism teaches that good and evil, the kingdom of God and the kingdom of Satan, develop simultaneously and grow until the end of this age. At the second coming of Christ the resurrection and judgment will take place followed by the new heaven and the new earth.

HOW SHALL WE EVALUATE THESE VIEWS?

1. Only God has the answers·to the many questions relating to the end of time. We must be content to leave the working out of details to him.

2. Our interpretation of the "millennium" is not a matter of our salvation. There are sincere biblical scholars identified with each of the three views.

3. We must be on our guard lest we become so fascinated with details that we miss the blessing of the message which the book is seeking to convey. We must also watch lest we adopt an attitude of dogmatic certainty which says, "This is the way things will happen. This is the order of events." It is almost certain that there will be surprises in store for all of us.

4. Perhaps the most widely held view is the amillennial view. According to Dr. Berkhof (*Systematic Theology*, p. 708), this view is as old as Christianity. Since the early years of the church it has been the view most widely accepted and is the only view that is either expressed or implied in the great historical confessions of the church.

OTHER DETAILS

The binding of Satan for a thousand years (Rev. 20:1-3) is interpreted by *amillennialists* to mean that Christ's death and resurrection broke the power of Satan. He is bound now in the lives of Christians to the degree that by God's grace they yield their lives to the control of the Holy Spirit (Rev. 12:11). Satan's power is curbed not only in the lives of Christians, but also in the world, through Christian witness and service. *The first resurrection* is referred to in Revelation 20:4-6. The *amillennial* view does not hold that there are two resurrections, but one general resurrection of all the dead when Christ comes again. The first resurrection referred to in this passage is interpreted to mean that when a Christian dies he is spiritually resurrected and is with Christ. Some believe that this passage refers especially to the martyrs. While the church continues on earth the martyrs reign with Christ. Others hold that the first resurrection refers to the time when a person becomes a Christian, for then he comes alive in Christ and is seated with him in the heavenly places (Eph. 2:6).

Satan is loosed from his prison when the thousand-year period is over (Rev. 20:7-10). Some interpreters believe that toward the end of the church age a time of severe trouble and persecution will break out on the earth when Satan will muster all the enemies of the church in a last attempt to eliminate the Christian and defeat Christ. He deceives nations into believing that he is able to do this. The names *Gog* and *Magog*, taken from Ezekiel 38 and 39, came to symbolize the enemies of God and his people. Satan leads his army in a last great onslaught on the "camp of the saints and the beloved city" (Rev. 20:9). Amillennialists do not interpret this literally to mean Jerusalem, but believe it means the last attack on the church. The battle mentioned here seems to be the battle of Armageddon referred to in Revelation 16:16 and Revelation 19:19. Whatever Scripture means by the term "Armageddon," it is fascinating to note that analysts of world affairs refer to another war as "Armageddon." George Wilson writing in the *Washington Post* a few years ago said, "The United States and the Soviet Union are on the verge of producing doomsday weapons that may so upset the present balance of terror that it can never be restored." The late General Douglas MacArthur writing about all the failures of peace efforts stated, "We have had our last chance. If we will not devise some greater and more equitable system, Armageddon will be at the door."

None of the references in the Revelation to Armageddon describe the battle itself. Each concentrates on the victory of Christ. When all the forces of evil, all the antagonists, are gathered to do battle with Christ and his people, then Christ, the mighty warrior, will appear and consume them with the breath of his mouth, with his Word of power. Then Satan will be thrown into hell, chained forever, nevermore able to harass and persecute the children of God.

The judgment at the great white throne (Rev. 20:11-15). Those who interpret this chapter literally believe that this judgment is only for the lost and that it occurs after the thousand-year-period is over. Others, including *amillennialists*, believe that all men, both saved and lost, are included in this judgment. Every person who has ever lived will be resurrected to stand before the judgment seat of Christ.

For the Christian, his judgment in relation to his eternal salvation is already past; his name has been written in the Lamb's book of life. Jesus said, "Truly, truly, I say to you, he who hears my word and believes him who sent me, has eternal life; he does not come into judgment, but has passed from death to life" (John 5:24). What a comfort to know that a person does not have to wait until the judgment day to know whether or not he belongs to God! He may have the glad certainty right now that he possesses eternal life. "He who *has* the Son *has* life" (1 John 5:12). However, on that day, a Christian's life will be judged—evaluated—as to what he has done with the life God has given him. Passages such as 1 Corinthians 3:13-15, 2 Corinthians 5:10 and Revelation 20:12 seem to indicate this. Ultimately the life-style and what one's life produces is indicative of what or who is at the center of that life.

It is interesting to note that *heaven and earth fled away* from God upon the throne (Rev. 20:11). Creation was also corrupted by the sin of Adam and Eve, and so needs to be restored. Paul says that all of creation is on "tiptoe" (Phillips) waiting for Christ to return; then it will be released from its bondage to decay and will experience the "glorious liberty of the children of God" (Rom. 8:19-21). Creation must be cleansed, renovated, and restored. The Apostle Peter says, ". . . the heavens will be kindled and dissolved, and the elements will melt with fire! But according to his promise, we wait for new heavens and a new earth in which righteousness dwells" (2 Peter 3:12-13).

All the enemies of Christ and his people are not out of the way. Babylon, the beast, the false prophet, the devil, death, and Hades, and all whose names are not written in the "book of life"—all are thrown into the lake of fire. While it may appear that these enemies go down, one by one, we must remember that this is symbolic language and is not to be thought of as a chronological order. When Christ comes again, Satan and every enemy will be defeated once and for all.

ENCOURAGEMENT AND HOPE

These chapters reecho the keynote of the victory of Jesus Christ, the theme of the book of Revelation. This book was not written to satisfy curiosity or speculation about the future, but to give courage and hope. The contents of these chapters may puzzle us, but let us remember Jesus Christ is coming again, victorious over every enemy, coming to make all things new.

The "great white throne" before which we all must stand is a sobering thought. How reassuring to have the glad certainty that our names are "written in the book of life;" to know that, as we yield our lives to the control of the Holy Spirit, he is at work, bearing fruit through us.

What pain the words, "thrown into the lake of fire," must bring to the loving heart of God. He who in his love and wisdom had sought to draw men to himself, must now let them experience what they have chosen: exclusion from his presence. "O, may my heart be broken with that which breaks the heart of God."

81

Heaven rings with the hallelujahs of victory. When things seem dark and discouraging, join in spirit with those victorious songs of heaven and sing, "Praise God! Jesus is victor. He is King of kings and Lord of lords. Hallelujah!"

> Alleluia! sing to Jesus,
> His the sceptre, his the throne;
> Alleluia! his the triumph,
> His the victory alone.
> Hark! the songs of peaceful Sion
> Thunder like a mighty flood,
> 'Jesus out of every nation
> Hath redeemed us by his Blood.'

William Chatterton Dix 1837-98

XI. NEW PEOPLE IN A NEW WORLD

(Revelation 21:1—22:5)

The consummation toward which the book of Revelation has been moving, and toward which all of history is moving, is now before us. Pictured here in symbolic language is the beauty, joy, and blessedness which those who have followed the Lamb will enjoy with him eternally. These chapters are filled with new things, for God has said, "Behold, I make all things new" (Rev. 21:5). We see the new heaven and new earth, the new Jerusalem, a new people, and a new experience.

THE NEW HEAVEN AND THE NEW EARTH (Rev. 21:1-8)

In the first chapters of Genesis we have the account of the creation of the world, God making it a beautiful place for man, the crown of his creation. But when sin came into the world, all of creation was touched by the results of sin. When Christ returns, creation will be set free from its bondage to sin and decay (Rom. 8:21). Creation will be restored and renovated, cleansed to make way for the new creation, the new heaven and earth. What we see here in these chapters is beyond history. It is the experience of all the redeemed following the second coming of Christ, the resurrection and the judgment.

What a glorious prospect. We will be new people set free from all the sin, weakness, and limitations which plague us now, living in a new world from which all wrong and corruption have been removed, living together in love and joy, serving God eternally.

Torrance says in relation to this new experience: "The Garden of Eden meant that God has made man to have communion with him in a perfect environment, and that true human life is essentially life in such a perfect environment. Therefore the perfection of the Christian life involves the perfection of earth as well as heaven. The Christian hope is fulfilled only in a new heaven and a new earth peopled with human beings living in holy and loving fellowship with God, with one another, and in harmony with the fulness of creation."

God is planning the very best for his children, and the fulfillment will far surpass our greatest expectations. The reason that it will be perfect is that God is its author. It originates in heaven (Rev. 21:2). Man is working so hard to improve his world and its environment. Some day this world will be perfected, but only because God has made it so. It will be the perfect, permanent dwelling place for God's redeemed children.

How can we be sure that God is planning such a great future for us? Because he who has said that he will make all things new, is trustworthy and true (Rev. 21:5). We can depend upon his Word. He is the Alpha and the Omega, the beginning and the end. He has created this world with a purpose and he will fulfill his plan and bring it to completion. Therefore he can say, "It is done!" (Rev. 21:6) he is so certain that his purposes will be accomplished. We can be that certain too.

What comfort for tested and tried Christians living in a troubled world! God is in perfect control. He will bring history to an end and will usher in a new world prepared for his own. Therefore when dark clouds appear on the world's horizon, let the Christians keep this vision before them knowing that in Christ they have a bright future.

THE NEW CITY (Rev. 21:9—22:5)

The materialistic world pinned its hopes on its own city, Babylon. That has collapsed and is no more. In contrast we see the heavenly city, glorious in beauty. In contrast to the harlot we see the radiant bride of Christ, the church. John sees the Holy City, the New Jerusalem, coming down from heaven as a bride adorned for her husband (Rev. 21:2). John has described earlier (Revelation 19) the marriage supper of the Lamb which was soon to come. Now in this chapter the consummation finally takes place. Christ, the heavenly Bridegroom, comes again and is united eternally with his bride, the church.

The city which John describes here is not to be taken as the literal earthly city of Jerusalem. John goes beyond that. In the Spirit he is given a vision of the heavenly Jerusalem, the place which Jesus said he had gone to prepare for his own. John is using earthly language to help us understand the glory of the city "not made with hands." There is a mystery as to what the new Jerusalem will be like; so our resurrection bodies are not understandable to us now. But nonetheless, the heavenly Jerusalem will be a reality.

As John looks down upon the heavenly city from the top of a high mountain he seeks to tell us in symbolic language what the city is like. The first thing that John notices is that *it is a city of light*. The glory of God emanates from it so that it shines with the radiance of a diamond (Rev. 21:10-11). "God is light and in him is no darkness at all" (1 John 1:5). The presence of God fills the city with light and now that sin has been removed, God can dwell with his people and have perfect fellowship with them (Rev. 21:3). When God created the first world, he made the sun, moon, and stars to be its light. Here in his new creation, there is no longer any need for the sun and moon, "for the glory of God is its light and its lamp is the Lamb" (Rev. 21:23).

The city is a place of order, balance, and security, symbolized by the walls and gates (Rev. 21:12-13). No fear of exclusion; perfect security.

The city is founded upon the Word of God, that Word which was proclaimed by the Old Testament prophets and the New Testament apostles, symbolized by the names of the 12 tribes of Israel inscribed on the gates and the names of the 12 apostles on the foundation stones

(Rev. 21:12-14). These foundations are unshakeable; this city will last forever.

This city is large and spacious; there is room for all who would enter, symbolized by its measurements, twelve thousand stadia or 1500 miles in length, breadth and height (Rev. 21:16). This number is a product of 3 (God's number, the Trinity) multiplied by 4 (number of the earth or universe) times 1000 (the number of completeness). Thus this symbolic number indicates the vastness of the heavenly city and also that God's redemption has touched the whole universe.

The heavenly city is a place of exquisite beauty and radiance (Rev. 21:18-21). It seems as if John is groping for words to describe its splendor. The cube, which symbolizes the symmetry and perfection of the city, is made of pure gold, transparent as crystal (Rev. 21:18). Can you imagine transparent gold? Or picture the glory of God which fills the city shining out through the transparent gold? The wall of the city is made of jasper, thought to be a precious stone like the diamond. This city needs no wall to protect it from enemies, as did the ancient cities of John's day. But he is using an ancient city as a model to convey the meaning of the heavenly city.

A wall built of diamonds, the foundations of the wall adorned with precious stones, every gate a huge single pearl, streets of pure, transparent gold—all of this reflecting, radiating, enhancing the glory of God which fills the city—how better could John reveal to us the beauty, glory, radiance, and perfection of this eternal city?

This city is for the whole world (Rev. 21:24-26). "For God so loved the world that he gave his only Son that whoever believes in him should not perish (be excluded from the eternal city) but have eternal life," now as a present possession, and on that day, with God forever in the new city. This is an international city, for the nations walk in its light and the kings of the earth bring their glory to it. This city will be peopled by Christians from every nation, tribe and tongue—by all whose names are written in the Lamb's book of life.

The city is vibrant with life from the eternal God (Rev. 22:1-2). In the center of the city, in the city square, are a river and a tree. The river, limpid as crystal, flows out from the throne of God and of the Lamb, symbolizing eternal life which has its source in God. Jesus said concerning the life he gives, "If any one thirst, let him come to me and drink. . . . Out of his heart shall flow rivers of living water" (John 7:37-38). The life we experience in Christ now is a dynamic, vibrant, growing life. So, too, in eternity, it will not stagnate but continue to flow and grow because it is God's life in us. One writer says, "Eternal life is not fixing life in one instant that lasts forever; it is not immovable, unchangeable granite, not a frigid immobility, the fusion of everything into a great whole. It is evolution, vitality, a rapid renewal like a bubbling stream from the mountains, youth forever re-created by communion with him who is Life itself."

In the first garden which God created, there were two trees which had special significance, the tree of life and the tree of the knowledge of good and evil. After man had disobeyed God by eating from the forbidden tree, he was barred from access to the tree of life, lest his alienation from God be fixed forever. But now in this new garden we see the tree of life again. The Greek for this expression is "the wood of life." Hence, this tree is symbolic of the cross and the salvation which Jesus won for us by pouring out his life on that tree. Throughout eternity the presence of the "word of life" will cause our hearts to praise and thank him that his death made it possible for us to have a part in this beautiful city of life.

The tree of life bears fruit constantly, in its leaves is healing. The sons of Adam are no longer barred from eating of the tree, but can partake freely of its fruits, which symbolize the very life of Christ which will sustain and nourish us throughout eternity. All the fruits of sin are now healed through the fruit of the tree of life.

Absent from the beautiful city are the elements and conditions which plague us now and keep us from having perfect peace and joy. The absence of these conditions makes the city a glorious place of perfection.

What Conditions Will Be Eliminated from the Beautiful City?

No more tears (Rev. 21:4). As a mother stoops down and wipes the tears from her child's eyes, so God will wipe every tear from our eyes. There will be no more heartaches and disappointments which cause tears.

No more death. It is the separation caused by death which causes tears and sorrow, mourning, and crying. But now death is eliminated. There will be no more separation but a joyful, eternal companionship with those we love.

No more pain. What a blessed prospect for those who in this life have had to learn to live with pain, or for Christians who were tortured to the point of death! Free from pain forever—both physical and mental!

No more thirst (Rev. 21:6b). No more restless longings for something to satisfy the deep needs of the human heart. Jesus said to the Samaritan woman, "Whoever drinks of the water that I shall give him will never thirst" (John 4:14). The Christian experiences even now a deep inner contentment, but he longs for a deeper and more meaningful experience with Christ. In the New Jerusalem all these longings will be met; we will know Christ in all his fullness and continue to drink from the fountain of the water of life which is Christ himself.

No more darkness. There will be no night there (Rev. 21:25; 22:5). In our cities today the darkness of night is often a cover for crime. But all that will be eliminated from the eternal city. There will be no need for artificial lighting or for created luminaries, for God himself will light the city. (Rev. 22:5)

No more of ánything accursed (Rev. 22:3). When sin came into the world man and his world were touched with the curse of sin. The ground was cursed; thorns and thistles sprang up, and man was destined to make

86

his bread "in the sweat of his face." Throughout his life man is plagued by struggle and frustration. But all that will be over in the new city of God. The curse of sin will have been removed forever. Man will be set free to serve God perfectly in the service of worship. There will be no boredom in the heavenly city but ceaseless, joyful activity, worshiping God.

Who Will Be Excluded from the New Jerusalem (Rev. 21:8, 27)?

The cowardly. They are the ones who did not have the courage or strength to remain faithful to Jesus when suffering persecution.

The faithless. This may refer to those who gave up their faith in Jesus when tested by trials, or those who have never put their faith and trust fully in Christ.

The polluted. They are those who contaminated themselves by worshiping the beast and became ensnared by the enticements of the worldly city, Babylon.

Murderers, fornicators. This may refer to those who persecuted and killed Christians, or murderers in general. Fornicators may refer to those who committed spiritual adultery with the harlot, Babylon, or to impurity in general.

Sorcerers, idolaters. They are those whose religion has been centered in the occult, in witchcraft, astrology, or magic. Idolatry is putting anything in the place of God.

Liars. Those involved in any kind of falsehood, phoniness, hypocrisy, insincerity. God is a God of truth and hates falsehood.

The unclean or those who practice abomination. There will be no unholiness in the new Jerusalem.

Let us remember that there is forgiveness for all these sins; we are all sinners, but the people mentioned here are excluded from the glory because they have refused to humble themselves and seek God's gift of forgiveness in Christ. Therefore they must experience the second death, spiritual death, exclusion from the presence of God forever, from all that is good, beautiful, true, joyful, and glorious. What tragedy! And yet we can see the mercy of God even here, for heaven would be hell for these people. Jesus is the center of heaven and only those who love him will enjoy his presence. The enemies of God would be most miserable in his presence.

What Will Be the Crowning Glory of This New Experience?

It is to be in the very presence of Christ and have unbroken, perfect fellowship with him. The greatest joy in our Christian experience now is to sense the nearness of Christ and to find joy in his presence. But so often this experience fluctuates. In the heavenly home it will be constant with nothing to mar this fellowship, no cloud to hide his glorious face. He will live in the midst of his people; they will be his people and God himself will be with them (Rev. 21:3). "We are God's children now;

87

it does not yet appear what we shall be, but we know that when he appears we shall be like him for we shall see him as he is" (1 John 3:2). We will see his face and his name will be on our foreheads (Rev. 22:4). He will be the center of our thoughts, our love, our joy.

Worship will be perfected in the heavenly city. The Temple had been a very important place in Jewish worship, with its sacrificial system. The church today has but one function—to assist us in our worship of God. But in the heavenly Jerusalem there will be no temple (Rev. 21:22); there will be no need of a temple, for God and the Lamb are the temple. We will need nothing to assist us in our worship for we will have direct access to God; the gates will never be closed (Rev. 21:25).

> "Eye hath not seen, nor ear heard,
> Neither have entered into the heart of man,
> the things which God hath prepared for them that love him"
> (1 Cor. 2:9). Amen.

Jerusalem the golden,
  With milk and honey blest,
Beneath thy contemplation
  Sink heart and voice oppressed;
I know not, O I know not
  What joys await us there,
What radiancy of glory,
  What bliss beyond compare.

O sweet and blessed country,
  The home of God's elect!
O sweet and blessed country,
  That eager hearts expect!
Jesus, in mercy bring us
  To that dear land of rest,
Who art, with God the Father
  And Spirit, ever blest. Amen.

Bernard of Cluny, XII cent.

Tr. John Mason Neale, 1818-66

XII. HE IS COMING SOON

(Revelation 22:6-21)

We have now come to the last segment in the book of Revelation, the epilogue. In the preceding lesson we viewed the beautiful, eternal city which awaits all who love God and have been faithful to the Lamb. Everything that was lost in the first Paradise in Eden, we see restored in the second Paradise of the heavenly Jerusalem.

Now the visions which were given to John are over. Before he closes his book there are certain truths which he seeks to impress upon his readers. These important truths come to us through three voices, that of an angel, of John, and of Jesus himself. At times it is difficult to ascertain who is speaking, perhaps because we are to realize that regardless of who speaks, it is really the voice of Jesus that comes to us in this whole book.

JOHN WISHES TO IMPRESS THESE TRUTHS UPON HIS READERS

1. *The authenticity of the book and John's authority in writing it.* The *angel affirms* the genuineness of the book, saying that the words of the Revelation are trustworthy and true because they have come from God himself. He is the One who has guided the spirit of the prophets (Rev. 22:6). John is repeating here what he said at the outset of the book: God is the author.

Next *John verifies* the fact that it was he, John, well known to the churches in Asia Minor, who had received these visions (Rev. 22:8).

Finally, *Jesus himself attests* to the validity of the contents of the Revelation. It was he who had sent his angel with the message to the churches (Rev. 22:16). He testifies that all these things which have been written are true (Rev. 22:20).

2. *The relevancy of the book of Revelation.* The book is not to be sealed up because the time is near (Rev. 22:10). Rather, it is to be open so that it can be read, for it has a message which is always contemporary. While the book grew out of the difficult situation in which the first century Christians found themselves, a situation where emperor worship was demanded at the threat of death, it has a message for Christians in any period of history. Therefore the time is always near. The Christian must ever heed the message of this book to be loyal to Christ no matter what the cost.

3. *The seriousness of rejecting the message of Christ* (Rev. 22:11). It has been said, "The same sun that hardens bricks melts butter." One's relationship with Christ depends on one's willful response to him. Each time a person says "no" to the appeal of Christ, a hardening sets in. If

one continues saying "no," a time may come when he cannot say "yes." Christ does not force anyone to follow him. He respects the dignity of the human will. Thus we read, "Let the evil doer still do evil and the filthy still be filthy." He is free to make his own choice; but one day that choice will be fixed beyond repair. On that day he will find himself outside the gates of the heavenly city (Rev. 22:15), in the company of all those who have loved their own way of life and have refused the love of Christ. The greatest tragedy is that there will no longer be opportunity for repentance on that day—only eternal exclusion from the presence of Christ.

By the same token, each time a person says "yes" to Christ, each time he surrenders to the promptings of the Holy Spirit, his relationship with Christ will become more firm and fixed so that the righteous will "still do right and the holy still be holy"—until that day.

4. *The blessedness of those who heed the message of the book.* There are seven beatitudes in the book of Revelation. The first one contains a blessing for those who read, hear, and keep what is written in this prophecy (Rev. 1:3). Other beatitudes give hope to Christians to persevere in difficult times. The last two beatitudes are stated in the final segment of the book. The sixth beatitude is directed to the individual —not to the church as a whole—but to the one who keeps the message of this book (Rev. 22:7b).

The seventh beatitude speaks of the blessedness of those who have washed their robes so that they are ready and prepared for the heavenly city (Rev. 22:14).

God has provided in Christ all that man needs to wash his robes. In his death and resurrection Christ has offered forgiveness and salvation to all. But as Barclay says, "Man has to wash his own robes in the blood of Jesus Christ." That is, he must appropriate all that God has done for him; he must make it his own by opening his heart to Christ (Rev. 3:20). When Jesus said, "I am the bread of life" he indicated that he is to be "eaten," assimilated into all of life. The one who has the life of Christ dwelling in him is prepared to enter the city by the gates.

5. *The seriousness of tampering with the message of this book* (Rev. 22:18-19). It has always been a temptation for those who study the Revelation to set dates, make dogmatic predictions, and see in contemporary world events a positive fulfillment of the Revelation. The book was not written to provide material for wild speculations.

There is another danger, that of shunning the book altogether, denying its importance or its divine authorship. The warning is directed against those who add to, or take away from, the words of this prophecy. It may refer to those who manipulate this book to make it fit their own particular scheme of eschatology. The severity of the judgment described in these verses is to impress on the reader the seriousness of tampering with this book.

6. *The urgency of the message in the Revelation.* Three times in these closing verses Jesus says, "I am coming soon" (Rev. 22:7, 12, 20), im-

plying that he may come at any time. The first century Christians looked for him to come in their generation. Because he has delayed his coming so long, many tend to overlook this great event or to say, as did the scoffers in Peter's day, "Where is the promise of his coming? For ever since the fathers fell asleep, all things have continued as they were from the beginning of creation" (2 Peter 3:3-4). Peter reminds his readers that the reason Christ is delaying his coming is that he is forbearing, "not wishing that any should perish, but that all should reach repentance" (2 Peter 3:9). Jesus sounded this same note of urgency in the Gospels when he said, "Watch therefore, for you do not know on what day your Lord is coming. Therefore you also must be ready; for the Son of man is coming at an hour you do not expect" (Matt. 24:42, 44). The appearing of the heavenly Bridegroom is the event for which his bride, the church, is longing and waiting. Therefore, we should respond, "Come, Lord Jesus!"

7. *The open invitation to come to Christ* (Rev. 22:17). In view of the judgments which will fall on those who reject Christ, and the beautiful future which is in store for those who love Christ, John cannot close without extending a final appeal to all who have not made use of the present opportunity to come to Christ. Christ has not yet come; the door of salvation is still open. When he returns, the opportunity to enter will be closed. "The Spirit and the bride say, 'Come.'" The Holy Spirit, through the Word and preachers of that Word, extends the invitation. The bride, the church, through its witnessing says, "Come." All who have heard and responded say, "Come."

What are the requisites for accepting this invitation? *To be thirsty, to desire* the water of life, and *to take* it freely. Isaiah calls out the same invitation when he says, "Ho, every one who thirsts, come to the waters; and he who has no money, come, buy and eat!" (Isa. 55:1). What simple requirements these are and yet how profound!

First, to thirst, to sense a need and a vacuum within, which only that which is of the Spirit can fill.

Next, to desire the water of life, to really want Christ and to believe that he can satisfy the deep longings of the human heart. The world has provided a variety of ways by which man seeks to fill this vacuum, but he must reject these ways and be willing to explore Christ's way.

Finally to take the water of life. He must come boldly to Christ, open to him, appropriate him. To all who open the door, he promises, "I will come in and fellowship with him and he with me" (Rev. 3:20, *Living Letters*). All who have heeded this gracious invitation are ready for his coming. Thus they can say together with the Spirit and the bride, "Come, Lord Jesus" and live in joyful expectation of his coming.

TRUTHS TO BE TREASURED

We have come to the close of our study of the Revelation. As we think through the book there are certain truths and highlights which we would like to remember. Perhaps these questions will assist in impressing these highlights on your hearts:

1. *Has your view or concept of Christ been enlarged?*

Have you seen him in all his resurrection glory, holding the destiny of the world in his hands, in perfect control of history, conquering every enemy, and finally bringing history to a close as he returns as the victorious King of kings and Lord of lords? Have you seen him as the concerned Friend, walking in the midst of his church, encouraging, exhorting, warning; or as the Lamb who is in reality, the Shepherd, comforting his persecuted children and leading them home where he will fellowship with them in the new Jerusalem?

2. *Have you understood the meaning of true worship?*

We have seen that the worship of heaven is joyful, directed toward the triune God; it is full of praise for all that God is; it is full of thanksgiving for all that God has done in his work of creation and redemption; it is full of love for Jesus who gave his life that we might have life; it grows out of the Word of God, is Spirit-produced and fills the heart with song. We see, too, that true worship may flow from an anguished heart that cries, "How long, oh Lord?" Or it may not be able even to find words; a deep groan from the depths of one's spirit may be the only expression possible. Surely this must have been so in the experience of the many persecuted and martyred Christians. True worship then, is the heart of man reaching out to the heart of God, whether in joy or in sorrow.

3. *Have the songs of the book made you aware of the many hymns and other great music which have been inspired by the Revelation?*

Find the following numbers from the *Messiah:* "Behold the Lamb of God" (Revelation 5); "But who may abide the day of his coming? and who shall stand when he appeareth? He is like a refiner's fire." (This theme runs throughout the series of judgments in Revelation 6, 8, 9, and 16). "For Unto Us a Child Is Born" (Revelation 12); the "Hallelujah Chorus" (Rev. 11:15 and 19:1-6); and the final chorus from the *Messiah,* "Worthy Is the Lamb," "Blessing and Honor" and the final "Amen" (Revelation 5). What masterpieces of art have been inspired by the Revelation?

4. *Have the sufferings and trials depicted in the book caused you to examine the quality of your own faith?*

Do you want to be more loyal to Christ, no matter what the cost, knowing that loyalty to him means triumph now and forever?

5. *Have you become more aware of the role which Satan plays in the world scene and of the subtle ways by which he tries to influence people to follow "Babylon"?*

Have you been encouraged to know that he is a defeated enemy and that through your union with Christ, you, too, have victory over him? (Remember Rev. 12:11.)

6. *Has your heart been gripped and burdened by the realization that there are many people who have refused to follow the Lamb and have been seduced by the wiles of the harlot, Babylon, and will have to suffer the terrible judgments of the wrath of God and be shut out forever from the beautiful city of God?*

Will you tell them that the door is still open? Will you urge them to drink of the water of life while it is still "today"?

7. *Does the vision of the new heaven and earth fill your heart with joy, expectation, and longing for that day when we shall stand in the very presence of Jesus, rejoicing in all the beauty and glory that he has prepared for us, in fellowship with him and with one another eternally, when a thousand years will be as a day and a day as a thousand years?*

When he says, "I am coming soon," does your heart respond eagerly, "Come, Lord Jesus!"

"Maranatha!"   "Come, Lord Jesus!"

"The grace of the Lord Jesus be with all the saints. Amen"

Our hope and expectation,
O Jesus, now appear;
Arise, thou Sun so longed for,
O'er this benighted sphere!
With hearts and hands uplifted,
We plead, O Lord, to see
The day of earth's redemption
That brings us unto thee! Amen.

Laurentius Laurenti, 1660-1722
Tr. Sarah Borthwick Findlater, 1823-1907

BIBLIOGRAPHY

For the Letters to the Seven Churches (Revelation 2, 3)

J. Campbell Morgan, *A First Century Message to Twentieth Century Christians*, Revell, 1902.

John R. Stott, *What Christ Thinks of the Church*, Eerdmans, 1958.

Henry B. Swete, *The Apocalypse of St. John*, Macmillan, 1917.

Richard C. Trench, *The Epistles to the Seven Churches*, Scribner, 1872.

The Pulpit Commentary, *Revelation*, Funk and Wagnalls.

For the Book of Revelation

Barclay, William, *The Revelation of John*, Vol. 1 and 2, Philadelphia: Westminster, 1959.

Beckwith, Isbon T., *The Apocalypse of John*, New York: Macmillan, 1919; reprinted, Grand Rapids: Baker, 1967.

Caird, G. B., *The Revelation of St. John the Divine*, New York: Harper, 1966.

Ellul, Jacques, *The Meaning of the City*, Grand Rapids: Eerdmans, 1970.

Gettys, Joseph M., *How to Study the Revelation*, Richmond: John Knox, 1963.

Glasson, T. F., *The Revelation of John* (Cambridge Bible Commentary), Cambridge: University Press, 1965.

Hendriksen, W., *More Than Conquerors*, Grand Rapids: Baker, 1940.

Kallas, James, *Revelation: God and Satan in the Apocalypse*, Minneapolis: Augsburg, 1973.

Ladd, George Eldon, *A Commentary on the Revelation of John*, Grand Rapids: Eerdmans, 1972.

Lilje, Hanns, *The Last Book of the Bible*, Philadelphia: Fortress Press, 1957.

Morgan, G. Campbell, *The Unfolding Message of the Bible*, Old Tappan: Revell, 1961.

Morris, Leon, *Apocalyptic*, Grand Rapids: Eerdmans, 1972.

Poellot, Luther, *Revelation*, Saint Louis: Concordia, 1962.

Rist, Martin, *Revelation, The Interpreter's Bible*, Vol. 12, Nashville: Abingdon, 1957.

Schlink, M. Basilea, *World in Revolt*, Minneapolis: Bethany Fellowship, 1969.

Tenney, Merrill C., *Interpreting Revelation*, Grand Rapids: Eerdmans, 1957.

Torrance, Thomas F., *The Apocalypse Today*, Grand Rapids: Eerdmans, 1959.

SUGGESTED THEME VERSE: "Blessed is he who reads aloud the words of the prophecy, and blessed are those who hear, and who keep what is written therein; for the time is near" (Rev. 1:3).

ACKNOWLEDGEMENTS

[1] *Apocalyptic*, Leon Morris, Eerdmans.

[2] *More Than Conquerors*, W. Hendricksen, Baker Book House.

[3] *The Last Book of the Bible*, Hanns Lilje, Fortress Press.

Quotations from above used by permission.

LESSON 1
THE VICTORIOUS LORD IS ALIVE
REVELATION 1

INTRODUCTION TO THE STUDY

The book of Revelation has been a closed book for many people for much too long. Perhaps most people do not realize God is so eager that this book be studied that he has promised a special blessing to all who read and heed its message.

1. Read Rev. 1:3. Memorize this verse, appropriate the promise, expect and thank God for the blessings which will come to you through this study.

2. Read Rev. 1:1-3.

   a. Who is the real author or source of the Revelation?

   What difference should this make in your attitude toward studying this book?

   b. What other encouragements and motivations for studying Revelation do you find in Rev. 1:1-3?

3. In order to understand the background of the Revelation, review these items *briefly:* the historical background, the purpose, and the

characteristics of the writing. Look at the chart on page 5. The book begins with a vision of the risen, glorified Christ in chapter 1 and concludes with a vision of the new heaven and earth and a promise that Christ will come again. In between these visions all of history is depicted. Note the three series of judgments in chapters 6, 8-9, and 16 which symbolize the struggle between the church and the world, between Christ and Satan, and the judgment of God on the evil, unrepentant world. Note too, that before each judgment God encourages his children by permitting them to look into heaven and see there the joy and victory of those who have lived and died faithful to Christ. Finally, we see Christ defeating every enemy and fellowshipping with his children in the new heaven and earth.

THE GREETING
(Read Rev. 1:4-5a)

1. To whom is John addressing his writing?

2. The greeting is from the Holy Trinity (v. 4-5a). What is stated about each member of the Trinity? (The number 7 symbolizes perfection or fullness.)

3. Why did John use these descriptions of God, the Holy Spirit, and Christ in his greeting? Look at each description again. How would each bring courage and hope to persecuted Christians living under a pagan dictator who demanded to be worshiped as God?

98

THE ADORATION OF CHRIST
(Read Rev. 1:5b-7)

1. Underline in your Bible the words which describe Christ's relationship with his children.

2. Note the tense of the verbs — the past, present, and future. What is the significance of these tenses?

3. According to Rev. 1:6, who are these Christians who at times perhaps felt so insignificant compared with mighty Rome?

4. What encouragements would all these verses about Christ and his children (Rev. 1:5b-7) bring to suffering first century Christians?

5. What encouragement would v. 8 bring to them?

THE VISION OF CHRIST
(Read Rev. 1:9-16)

1. Answer these questions in relation to John's experience: (vv. 9-11)
Where was John? (Locate on the map)
Why was he there?

What happened?

What was he commanded to do? (Try to put yourself in John's place — a pastor banished to a lonely island. What may have been his thoughts and feelings that Sunday morning?)

2. How does John identify with the suffering Christians to whom this book was addressed (v. 9)? What encouragement would this bring to them?

3. Put in your own words what John's vision of Christ in Rev. 1:12-16 tells us about our exalted Lord.

4. What was the purpose of this vision? What would it mean to a small band of harried, frustrated Christians who perhaps at times were tempted to discouragement?

JOHN'S REACTION TO THE VISION
(Read Rev. 1:17-20)

1. What was John's reaction? What caused it?

2. Meditate on Jesus' answer to John (v. 17b-18). Read it over several times. Memorize these verses. What encouragement would these words bring to suffering first century Christians?

OUR RESPONSE

1. Many Christians today are losing heart because of conditions in the world which seem insolvable and hopeless. What encouragement does this chapter give?

2. Choose one verse or a part of a verse from this chapter which was meaningful to you personally. Thank God for the encouragement or truth you found in that verse, quoting the verse in your prayer, if you wish.

LESSON 11

CHRIST IS CONCERNED FOR HIS CHURCH

REVELATION 2 & 3

In Lesson One, the first vision is given to John. He sees the living Lord of the church standing in the midst of seven golden lampstands which represent the seven churches of Asia. Jesus instructs John to write what he sees, "What is and what is to take place hereafter." He also gives John a message for each of the seven churches. In this lesson we will study these messages which contain important truths applicable to the church of our day.

CHRIST'S MESSAGE TO THE SEVEN CHURCHES

Please complete the material on the chart on the next page. Read the background material on pages 16-17 about the first church, Ephesus; next read the biblical passage relating to that church. Then fill in the spaces on the chart which relate to Ephesus. Proceed to the next church and follow this procedure until you have completed the chart. You may wish to make a larger chart to have more room for writing. Note that a pattern is followed in each message. For some churches there is no rebuke; for others, no commendation—for all, a promise!

CHURCH	CHRIST'S TITLE	COMMENDATION	REBUKE	ADVICE & WARNING	PROMISE
EPHESUS					
SMYRNA					
PERGAMUM					
THYATIRA					
SARDIS					
PHILADELPHIA					
LAODICEA					

CHRIST'S MESSAGE TO HIS CHURCH TODAY

Point out some highlight about each church or Christ's admonition to it.

1. CHRIST LOOKS FOR LOVE (Ephesus) Read Rev. 2:1-7.
What is meant by "the love you had at first"?

What causes one to lose the glow of this first love?

Why does Jesus place such high value on this love?

2. CHRIST LOOKS FOR FAITHFULNESS (Smyrna) Read Rev. 2:8-11.
If you knew that a time of testing and persecution were coming when loyalty to Christ could mean suffering, or even death, how would you prepare your children or yourself for wholehearted allegiance to Christ?

3. CHRIST LOOKS FOR AN UNCOMPROMISING STAND FOR TRUTH (Pergamum) Read Rev. 2:12-17.
Do you think we are too tolerant of religions which deny the diety of Christ, the true meaning of the atonement, personal sin and other basic tenets of Christianity? If so, what is the reason for this? The remedy?

4. CHRIST LOOKS FOR AN UNCOMPROMISING STAND AGAINST EVIL (Thyatira) Read Rev. 2:18-29.
What situations do Christians face today which tempt them to compromise their convictions in order to be accepted? to avoid ridicule? or to succeed? What is the secret of achieving boldness in witnessing for Christ?

5. CHRIST LOOKS FOR SPIRITUAL LIFE (Sardis) Read Rev. 3:1-6.
Who is a spiritually alive person?

What are the marks of a spiritually alive church?

6. CHRIST LOOKS FOR A VITAL PROGRAM OF EVANGELISM (Philadelphia) Read Rev. 3:7-13.

What are some opportunities for outreach which your church is neglecting?

Recall a meaningful experience you have had in witnessing for Christ.

7. CHRIST LOOKS FOR A BURNING ZEAL (Laodicea)
Read Rev. 3:14-22.

Many feel that of all the churches, this one is most like the church of today. What characteristics of this church may lead to this conclusion?

What are the marks of a lukewarm Christian?

Why is it better that a person be cold or hot rather than being lukewarm? Wherein is Rev. 3:20 the answer to that which is lacking in the church in Laodicea and in all the churches?

According to Rev. 3:20 how can you be sure that Christ is living in your heart?

OUR RESPONSE

Choose one of the following prayers or use one of your own which has grown out of this study.

- Lord Jesus, thank you for your great love for me. Flood my heart with your love so that I may love you as I should.

- Lord, I admit that I know very little about suffering for your sake and it frightens me to think about it. Make me strong, O Lord, so that I will be true to you whatever the cost.

- O God, it's so easy to compromise my convictions and my actions because of what others will say or think. Please forgive me. Help me to be more bold in my witness for you.

- O God, sometimes my spiritual life seems dead. O Holy Spirit, come and fill my heart and make me truly alive.

LESSON III

CHRIST HOLDS THE DESTINY OF THE WORLD IN HIS HANDS

REVELATION 4 & 5

INTRODUCTION TO THE STUDY

1. Consult your chart and note that chapters 1-5 serve as a preparation of God's people for the judgments which follow. Review the first two lessons. How does chapter 1 serve as a preparation?

What encouragements for the suffering children of God are found in chapter 1?

How do chapters 2 and 3 prepare the church to be steadfast and victorious in persecution and judgment?

2. Read chapter III, pages 26-30.

3. Chapters 4 and 5 give added encouragement and hope as the curtain of heaven is drawn aside and the persecuted child of God is permitted to see the glory of God on the throne of the universe, and Jesus, the Lamb, in perfect control of the destiny of the world.

Read through chapters 4 and 5 for general impressions. Try to capture the mood of these chapters.

What do you see?

What do you hear?

What emotions do you experience?

4. What is the focal point of chapter 4?
of chapter 5?

GOD ON THE THRONE OF THE UNIVERSE
Revelation 4

1. As John looks into heaven he sees One upon a throne. God is not described but "he appeared like. . . ." How are God's glory and power symbolized in vv. 3 and 5?

2. Read Rev. 4:4-8. Try to reconstruct in your mind what John saw. At the center is a throne. Who surround the throne?

Who are they?

What is in front of the throne?

Who are on each side of the throne?

What do they represent? (See page 27.)

3. Read Rev. 4:8b-11. According to the song, why is God worthy to be praised?

4. Be quiet for a few moments. Close your eyes. Visualize the scene as a whole: a throne in heaven, and on it the God of the universe—effulgent in glory, radiance, beauty, power and holiness. Listen to the glorious music of the whole company of heaven as they sing the

song of creation to the One upon the throne. Take your place among them. Worship and adore your God.

5. With this vision before the eyes of your hearts, sing this stanza from a familiar hymn:

"Holy, holy, holy! All the saints adore thee,
     Casting down their golden crowns around the glassy sea.
Cherubim and seraphim falling down before thee,
     Which wert, and art, and evermore shall be."

6. What do you suppose this vision meant to the Christians of John's day, living under the Emperor Domitian who also was surrounded by great splendor and demanded to be worshipped as God?

THE DESTINY OF THE WORLD
IS IN THE HANDS OF THE LAMB
Revelation 5

1. Chapters 4 and 5 are a unit and present one vision. What does chapter 5 add to the scene in heaven?

2. Read Rev. 5:1-6.

a. Summarize your understanding of the meaning of the scroll in the hands of the Lamb.

b. What caused John such great sorrow?

c. What comfort did one of the elders give him?

3. Read Rev. 5:6-10.

a. What is the meaning of the symbolic description of the Lamb?

b. What follows when the Lamb takes the scroll from the hand of God?

c. According to the song in vv. 9 and 10, why is the Lamb worthy to be praised?

d. Usually the symbol of strength is a lion. What is the significance of the fact that Jesus is pictured as a lamb in the Revelation?

4. Read Rev. 5:11-14. Another group of singers is introduced, encircling the throne.

a. Who are they?

How many are there?

b. Underline in your Bible the seven-fold honor ascribed to the Lamb in their song (v. 12). What is the significance of the fact that there are 7 words mentioned?

c. Now the group is enlarged even more. What do these added singers represent?

Close your eyes and visualize the glory and beauty of this scene in heaven. Thank Christ for what he has done for you.

YOUR RESPONSE

1. Think about the message of these two chapters. How would you relate this message to people today who are worried and fearful because of the many serious situations in our troubled world?

2. Use the message of these chapters to enrich your worship experience. As you take part in a worship service, visualize that throng of worshippers in heaven and join them in their worship of the Lamb.

LESSON IV

GOD KEEPS HIS OWN SECURE

REVELATION 6 & 7

INTRODUCTION TO THE LESSON

Review previous lessons by consulting the chart (page 5). Note that the first division of the book, the PREPARATION (chapters 1-5) has now been completed.

From the first five chapters choose one idea or thought which tells how God encourages and prepares his people for the judgments which follow in succeeding chapters.

Chapter 1:   Chapter 4:

Chapters 2, 3:   Chapter 5:

THE SEALS ARE OPENED, JUDGMENT BEGINS

(Revelation 6)

Read chapters 6 and 7 being conscious of what you see, hear, and feel. Recall that in the previous lesson we saw the Lamb take from the hand of God the scroll of destiny which was sealed with seven seals. In this chapter, six of the seals are opened, revealing a tragic picture of world history. Keep remembering that the scroll is in the hands of the Lamb.

1. Read Rev. 6:1-8 and note the following about the four horsemen of the Apocalypse:

	Symbolic description	*Symbolic meaning*
Rider # 1		
Rider # 2		
Rider # 3		
Rider # 4		

2. There has been much discussion as to the identity of the first rider. Who do you think he represents? (See p. 31.)

3. Read Rev. 6:9-11. This scene, which shifts from earth to heaven, pictures the Christian martyrs.

a. What do they ask?   Why?

b. What is meant by God's answer to them?

4. The events related to the first five seals have always been a part of human history and always will be. What relevance do you see to things happening today?

5. Read Rev. 6:12-17, an apocalyptic description of the end time. While on earth Jesus used similar descriptions. (See Mark 13:24, 25.)

a. Note seven areas of nature which are affected.

b. Note seven classes of people.

c. These represent all who have rejected Christ. What causes their fear (vv. 16-17)?

d. A lamb is considered the most gentle and harmless of animals. Yet here we read of the "wrath of the Lamb," also referred to as the "wrath of love." What is meant by this wrath of the Lamb? (v. 16.)

e. This scene pictures the terror and despair of those who have refused the claim of Christ on their lives. Now the full realization dawns on them—all that Christ said was true, and now they must experience his rejection rather than his love. What tragedy! Pause for a few moments of silent prayer for those who have neglected or rejected Christ. Perhaps there is someone for whom you are especially concerned.

GOD KEEPS HIS OWN SECURE
(Revelation 7)

Six seals have been opened and now we would expect to see the seventh opened and Christ to appear immediately. But instead there is an interlude (chapter 7), the purpose of which is to give encouragement to God's children before the next series of judgments are revealed.

1. Read Rev. 7:1-3. This vision which John sees on earth symbolizes God's perfect control. No destructive judgment (four winds) can come except by God's permission, and even in the midst of judgment, those utterly devoted to God (servants) are secure (sealed).

2. Read Rev. 7:4-12. These verses give the symbolic picture of the church of Jesus Christ. The first, the sealed followers of the Lamb on earth, are the church militant (Rev. 7:4-8); and the second are the victorious saints in heaven, the church triumphant (Rev. 7:9-17).

a. What other interpretations of the 144,000 have you encountered?

b. The important thing to consider here is the symbolic meaning of this vision. What encouragement would it bring to Christians going through the trials and tribulations of life?

3. Read Rev. 7:9-17. The group pictured here is so large that no one can count the number. Only God knows the exact number of those who belong to him.

a. What words does John use to symbolize the *universality* of the group (v. 9)? What words to symbolize *victory?*

b. For what do they praise God (v. 10)?

c. What seven qualities do the angels ascribe to God (v. 12)?

d. Some people may feel that since they have done some heroic deed for Christ or suffered or even died for him, that on this basis Christ will welcome them to heaven. But what is the only thing that qualifies them to be in heaven (Rev. 7:14b)? Explain the meaning in your own words.

e. What is your understanding of the great tribulation (v. 14)?

f. What do you learn about heaven from vv. 15-17?

g. What do you look forward to most as you contemplate heaven?

SUMMARY CONTEMPLATION

As you read this segment describing heaven, perhaps the words of the hymn, "Behold a Host" came to mind. Read or sing this hymn. As you do so, thank God for the message of this chapter. Thank him that his loving eye is on you and that he will keep you secure in life and in death. Thank him for the reality of heaven and for all those who are now rejoicing before his throne.

LESSON V

THE PRAYERS OF CHRISTIANS MOVE THE HAND OF GOD

REVELATION 8 & 9

INTRODUCTION TO THE STUDY

1. Consult the chart, page 5. Note that we are in the second division of the book of Revelation which is titled "Conflict." In our last lesson we studied the first series of judgments, the seals. Recall the content of each of the six seals.

2. In this lesson we will study the second series of judgments, the trumpets. Many commentators feel that the three series of judgments depicted in the Revelation run parallel throughout history—that each series is a repetition of the previous series but with added features and looked at from a different perspective. Other commentators believe that the seals relate to all of history but that the trumpets and the bowls relate more specifically to the end of the age.

3. Read Revelation 8 and 9 to get a general idea of these chapters. What are your impressions and reactions?

PREPARATION FOR THE TRUMPET JUDGMENTS

1. Read Rev. 8:1-3. Note that the sixth seal introduces the trumpets.
a. Try to imagine yourself a part of that half hour's silence. What effect would it have? What purpose would it serve?

b. What does Rev. 8:3-5 tell us about the importance and power of prayer?

THE THREE JUDGMENTS

1. Read Rev. 8:6-12. Note the following about each of the first four trumpets:

	What happens	*The results*
1st		
2nd		
3rd		
4th		

2. What is the significance of the repetition of the phrase, *a third?*

3. Although these judgments are directed at the natural creation, how do they affect mankind? Do we see any of these effects today? (The figure of a trumpet, often an instrument of warning, is appropriate for what you see here.)

4. Read Rev. 8:13. According to the eagle's cry, at whom are the woes that follow directed? (See p. 38.)

THE FIFTH TRUMPET

1. Read Rev. 9:1-12. Who opens the bottomless pit?
What comes from the pit first?   Then what follows?

2. What were the locusts not permitted to do? Whom were the locusts permitted to torture for a limited time (5 months)?
Who are these people? (9:4b) Explain the meaning.
How does Rev. 9:6 indicate the severity of their torture?

3. Who is the leader of this demonic horde (9:11)?

4. This whole scene seems to picture in symbolic language demonic forces which plague those who reject Christ. It may also refer to the terrible evil of which man is capable when he refuses the power of the Gospel in his life and is thus under the power of sin and Satan. What evidences do you see of this in our world today?

THE SIXTH TRUMPET

1. Read Rev. 9:13-19. In what respect is the sixth trumpet judgment more severe than the fifth? (Think in terms of the demonic animals in each judgment and what they are permitted to do to godless mankind.)
2. The golden altar (9:13) reminds us again that God's people and their prayers are very important to God. He hears their cries and answers.
3. What does the symbolism of an exact time given for judgment (9:15) tell us about God and his judgments?

4. How large is this demonic cavalry (v. 16)?
How large a part of mankind was killed?

5. What words describe the ferociousness, power and demonic origin of the horses?

6. An encouraging note in these chapters is that God is in control and has greater power than Satan. But man, through his rebellion, makes it necessary for God to act. In each of the following verses, underline in your Bible the words which indicate that evil can exert itself only in limited ways: Rev. 9:3, 4, 5, 15.

THE PURPOSE OF JUDGMENT

1. Read Rev. 9:20, 21. What is the reaction of the godless world to the trumpet judgments?

2. Note the things which they refuse to give up and of which they do not repent.

3. In view of these verses, what is God's purpose in permitting judgments to come upon this world? Wherein are they an expression of his love and concern for mankind?

4. Old Testament prophets often looked upon natural disasters as judgments from God and a call to repentance. Is there evidence that disasters cause men to turn to God today?

A CALL TO PRAYER

Remember this encouraging thought: God will silence all the choirs of heaven to listen to your prayer. What prayer concerns come to your mind as you think through these chapters? Write a few short prayers.

1.
2.
3.

LESSON VI

THE WORD OF GOD WILL TRIUMPH

REVELATION 10 & 11

INTRODUCTION TO THE STUDY

1. Consult the outline chart of the Revelation (p. 5). Note that we are in the second division of the book titled CONFLICT, and two series of judgments, the Seals and the Trumpets, have now been studied.

2. Look back over the chapters and note which scenes take place on earth and which in heaven.

3. Read Revelation 10 and 11 keeping in mind that these chapters can symbolize the preaching of the Word of God and its reception by a hostile world.

THE UNIVERSALITY OF THE WORD

1. Read Rev. 10:1-7. What words used to describe the mighty angel seem to indicate that he is closely associated with Christ and comes from the very presence of God?

2. How would this vision of the mighty angel, who covers the whole

world with a message from God, encourage Christians who were often ridiculed because they had faith in the Word of God?

3. What happens when the angel calls out (v. 3)?

What does John plan to do?

What is he told to do?

There has been much speculation as to the content of the seven thunders. The fact that the message was to be sealed and not written down seems to indicate that there are mysteries to which only God has the answers.

4. The angel swears by God so the readers can be sure the oath will be fulfilled. How is God described (Rev. 10:6)?

What is promised in the oath (v. 6-7)?

5. What encouragement would this description of God and the content of the oath bring to tested and tried Christians of any age?

THE EFFECT OF THE WORD

1. Read Rev. 10:8-11. What is John commanded to do?

What is the effect of obeying the command?

2. What is the symbolic meaning of this for John? (See p. 44 for help).

3. What lessons do verses 8-11 hold for anyone who wishes to bring God's Word to others?

THE WITNESS OF THE WORD

Chapter eleven is perhaps the most difficult chapter in the Revelation. Biblical scholars are not agreed on its interpretation, so we must not become discouraged if we cannot understand all the details.

1. Read Rev. 11:1-13. Note these details in the account:

a. What is John instructed to do (v. 1)?

What is he not to do (v. 2)?

b. Of what two Old Testament leaders do the two witnesses described in Rev. 11:5, 6 remind you?

c. What happens to the witnesses when their task is done?

Who is their enemy?

d. What is the reaction of the hostile world to the death of the witnesses (Rev. 11:9, 10)?

e. How does God vindicate his witnesses (Rev. 11:11, 12)?

f. How does the world react to the signs which accompany the resurrection of the two witnesses (v. 13)?

2. In this book and other sources, read about some possible interpretations of Rev. 11:1-13.

3. If we think of the two witnesses as symbolizing the church in its task of bringing the Word of God to a hostile world, what might the following symbolic descriptions tell about what should characterize the preaching and witness of the church:
sackcloth (Rev. 11:3)
olive trees (which produce oil for the lamps). (See Zech. 4:6)
lampstands

4. Think of instances in our generation where the voice of the witness has been silenced because his message brought "torment" to the hostile world, or of countries where the Enemy has tried to stamp out the witness of the church.

5. Have you ever experienced any suffering or rejection because of your witness for Christ?

Do you think that if we are true to the Word of God in our witnessing that we can expect to experience some measure of suffering (see John 15:18-21)?

THE TRIUMPH OF THE WORD

1. Read Rev. 11:14-19. As the seventh trumpet sounds we would expect another plague to follow, but instead John looks down the aeons of time and sees the final triumph of Christ.

a. Recall what followed the opening of the seventh seal (Rev. 8:1).

b. In contrast, what occurs when the seventh trumpet is sounded (Rev. 11:15)?

c. What is the theme of the heavenly chorus (v. 15)?

d. For what do the elders thank and praise God (v. 16-18)?

2. What encouragement would these verses bring to witnesses of any age?

CONTEMPLATE YOUR TRIUMPH IN CHRIST

God calls us to be faithful witnesses even though it may mean opposition, rejection, or even martyrdom. But God promises us a glorious victory if we are faithful to him—a triumph which will far outweigh any suffering we may have to endure for his sake.

Play a recording of the "Hallelujah Chorus" which was inspired by Revelation 11:15. As you listen, praise God for the triumph which Jesus Christ will bring to this world when he comes again. Thank him, too, that you may share his victory even now as you abide in him.

LESSON VII

THE DEVIL IS A DEFEATED FOE

REVELATION 12 & 13

INTRODUCTION TO THE STUDY

Glance at the outline chart of Revelation to see the movement of the book thus far.

Read chapters 12 and 13 for general impressions. Note the relation of chapters 12 and 13 to the other chapters in the second division of the book, titled, CONFLICT. These chapters give the underlying cause of the conflict. They also bring a strong encouragement to suffering Christians by assuring them that though it may seem as if the devil is winning the battle, he has been completely defeated by Jesus' victory at Calvary.

THE BIRTH OF THE CHILD – THE FOCUS OF THE CONFLICT

1. Read Rev. 12:1-6. Summarize the content of John's vision and note these details: the three characters in this drama; the evil aim of the dragon; God's victory over the dragon (v. 5, 6).

2. What is the symbolic meaning of this vision?

3. Think of instances in the life of Jesus when Satan tried to destroy him.

THE DEFEAT OF THE ENEMY

1. Read Rev. 12:7-12. Between whom is the war in heaven?

2. How is the defeat of Satan described (v. 8, 9) and what causes the great celebration in heaven (v. 10, 11)?

3. What effect does Satan's defeat have on him? (v. 12)

4. How is the devil showing his wrath and increasing his activity in our day?

VICTORY OVER THE ENEMY

1. Look over Rev. 12:7-12 again and note the names given to the devil and the way he attacks Christians.

2. What are some ways in which the devil perhaps tried to deceive and accuse the early Christians?

3. What encouragement would Rev. 12:11 bring to them?

4. How does the enemy try to accuse and deceive you?

5. According to Rev. 12:11, what is the three-fold way of getting victory over him?

6. Do you think it makes any difference whether we regard the devil as a personality or merely as evil in general? Why?

THE CONFLICT CONTINUES

1. Read Rev. 12:13-17. When the devil is not able to destroy the Messiah, on whom does he now pour his hatred (v. 13, 17)?

2. How is his attack on God's children symbolized (v. 15, 17)?

3. How is God's protection of his children symbolized (v. 14, 16)?

THE BEAST OUT OF THE SEA
Read Rev. 13:1-10

1. What statements about this beast indicate its close association with the dragon? (Compare 13:1 and 12:3)

Where does it get its power and authority (13:2b, 4)?

2. How does this beast try to imitate Christ (13:3)?

3. What words describe its defiance and hatred of God and Christians (Rev. 13:5-7)?

4. Underline in your Bibles the words which indicate that the beast's power and influence are limited by God (v. 5-7).

5. Who did the first century Christians (perhaps) see symbolized in this beast?

6. Note that in 13:8 the verb tense changes to the future, *will worship*, perhaps indicating that this beast is not to be limited to just the first century. Who are some other "beasts" and their systems, who have tried throughout history to eradicate Christianity?

7. Who will worship this beast (13:8)?

What will this mean for Christians (13:9, 10)?

THE BEAST OUT OF THE EARTH
Read Rev. 13:11-18

1. The second beast does not appear to be as ferocious as the first beast, but wherein lies the subtle danger (13:11)?

2. What is the aim of this beast (v. 12)?

How does it go about accomplishing its goal (v. 13-15)?

3. The beast is able to deceive *those who dwell on earth* (v. 14), an expression used in Revelation for the non-Christian world. What is the fate of those who refuse to worship the beast (v. 15)?

4. How does the second beast enforce worship of the first beast (v. 16, 17)?

What does this result in for Christians?

5. Six is the symbolic number of incompleteness and evil (see p. 9, resource book). Torrance, a commentator on the Revelation, says, "666 is the number of every attempt to organize the world in a form that appears marvelously Christian but is in reality anti-Christian." Can you think of any contemporary examples which would illustrate this statement?

6. The second beast is also called the false prophet (16:13; 19:20). There are many new religions on the scene today. What questions should one ask to determine whether a religion is truly Christian?

ENCOURAGEMENT FOR TESTED CHRISTIANS

These chapters impress on us the reality of the Enemy and of the work of Satan throughout history on the world scene. Every Christian knows the subtle attacks of the Enemy. But let every Christian know assuredly that the devil has been defeated—stripped of his power when Christ died on the cross. And let the Christian warrior use that cross as a sword against the Enemy, reminding him that he has been defeated by the blood of the Lamb.

LESSON VIII

SONGS OF VICTORY AWAIT THE FAITHFUL

REVELATION 14, 15 & 16

INTRODUCTION TO THE STUDY

1. Glance at the outline chart and note that we are still in the interlude that occurs between the trumpet judgments (Rev. 8 and 9) and the final series of judgments (Rev. 16).

2. Read Rev. 14-16 for general impressions. Note how God encourages and warns his people before the bowls of wrath are poured out.

THE NEW SONG

Read Rev. 14:1-5

The scene shifts to heaven and again we meet the 144,000. In chapter 7 they were on earth, the church militant. Here they are in heaven, the church triumphant. God has led them safely home and not one is missing!

1. What contrasts do you note between this scene and Rev. 12 and 13 in terms of what you *see, hear* and *feel?*

	Rev. 12, 13	Rev. 14:1-5
See		
Hear		
Feel		

125

2. What does the symbolism tell us about the redeemed in heaven?

About the music?

3. What meaning would this scene (Rev. 14:1-5) have for persecuted Christians on earth?

What meaning does it have for you today?

THE MESSAGE OF THE THREE ANGELS

Read Rev. 14:6-11
1. To whom does the first angel bring his message (vv. 6, 7)?

Recall the meaning of the expression "those who dwell on earth."
(See p. 39.)

What does the angel urge people to do before it is too late (v. 7)?

2. What does the second angel prophesy (v. 8)?
This will be described fully in Revelation 17 and 18.

3. The third angel pronounces judgment on those who worshiped the
beast and received its mark (vv. 9-11). How did their lives indicate
their allegiance to the beast?

4. What does the symbolic language of vv. 9-11 tell us about the
terrible fate of those who are eternally lost?

Do you believe that these words are true and that hell is an awful
reality? What effect should these words have on us?

(Certainly we should never joke about hell. It is too serious and
tragic a matter to take lightly.)

COURAGE AND HOPE FOR CHRISTIANS
Read Rev. 14:12, 13
1. What are Christians encouraged to do (v. 12)?
Why?

2. Contrast the blessedness of the redeemed (v. 13) with the fate of the lost (vv. 9-11). Note the contrast in the word *rest*. (v. 11 and v. 13)

HARVEST TIME
Read Rev. 14:14-20
1. Note that the final judgment takes place when the harvest is fully ripe. (Rev. 14:15, 18) What does this mean?

What causes the world to become ripe for judgment?

Does evil ripen along with the good?

2. Do you think America is ripening for judgment?
If so, what can we do to avert judgment? (See 2 Chron. 7:14)

3. Revelation 14:20 pictures symbolically the complete destruction of the earth. Four (earth's number) times four, multiplied by ten (number of completion) times ten, equals 1600 which symbolizes total destruction.

THE SONG OF MOSES AND THE LAMB
1. Read Rev. 15:1-4. Before the seven angels are permitted to pour out the last plagues, God gives his suffering church another encouraging view of the victorious saints in heaven.
   a. How had these martyrs really conquered the beast (v. 2)?

   b. Why is their song called the "Song of Moses and the Lamb"? How were their experiences similar to those of the Israelites under Pharoah?

   c. About what do the saints sing (vv. 3, 4)?

2. Read Rev. 15:5-8. This paragraph describes the seven angels who come from the very presence of the glory of God to pour out his wrath on the impenitent in a last effort to bring them to repentance.

THE BOWLS OF WRATH

1. Read Revelation 16 and note *where* each bowl is poured and the result.

Bowls	Where Poured	Result
1st		
2nd		
3rd		
4th		
5th		
6th		
7th		

2. Against whom are these plagues directed (vv. 2, 9, 10)?
What is the response (vv. 9, 11, 21)?

3. How may it be said that God is just in his judgments (vv. 5-7)?

4. The sixth bowl is different from the others. Note these details:
   a. From where do the demonic spirits come and what is their evil purpose (vv. 13, 14)?

   b. Note the words which refer to the day of the last battle (v. 14b). *Whose* day is it?
   What encouragement does this bring to us as we think about the last conflict between God and the forces of evil?

   c. What is the meaning of the words in v. 15 and why are they interjected here?

5. What words express the finality and the severity of the last plague (vv. 17-21)?

PRAYER CONCERNS
List prayer concerns which have grown out of the study of these chapters.

LESSON IX

ONLY TREASURES ROOTED IN CHRIST WILL LAST

REVELATION 17 & 18

INTRODUCTION TO THE STUDY

The book of Revelation and history itself is moving toward the close of the age when God will bring in the new heaven and the new earth. But first every enemy of Christ and his church must be removed.

1. Recall the enemies that have been mentioned in the Revelation thus far, and their symbolic meaning.

2. Read Revelation 17 and 18 which describe the character and destruction of Babylon—the godless world system. Note that in chapter 17 Babylon is depicted as a harlot and in chapter 18 as a city.

THE HARLOT BABYLON

1. Read Rev. 17:1-6. How does this description of Babylon indicate her great evil, and her hatred of Christians? Note her sins.

   a. What does the description of the woman's dress and appearance indicate about the godless world system?

b. What groups had she seduced (v. 2)?

c. On what was the woman seated (v. 3)? Where have you seen this beast before? Recall its symbolic meaning. (See p. 51.)

2. Read Rev. 17:7-14. These verses are perhaps the most difficult in the Revelation. (Try to answer the questions with the help of p. 66, and other materials.) Don't be discouraged if you cannot understand all the details.

a. How is the beast that carried the woman described (vv. 7, 8, 11)?
   What are some possible interpretations of the description of the beast? (See p. 66.)

b. What do the seven heads of the beast symbolize (vv. 9, 10)?
   What are some possible interpretations of this symbolism?

c. What is the symbolic meaning of the ten horns (v. 12)?
   What is their relationship to the beast (v. 13)?

d. Pick out the expressions which indicate that God is in perfect control and that he limits the rule of the beast to a brief period (vv. 10, 12).

e. Rev. 17:14 looks toward the end when all the forces of evil will unite against Christ and his followers. How may we be certain that the Lamb will be victorious? (Note his title.)

f. How do the words which describe the followers of the Lamb (v. 14) indicate their dependence on him?

3. Read Rev. 17:15-18, describing the judgment on the harlot.

a. How is the extent of the harlot's influence and empire indicated (v. 15)?

b. How will the devotees of the harlot treat her (v. 16)?

c. How does v. 17 show that God is in control and that his purposes will be carried out?

4. The first century Christians perhaps saw in the symbolic description of the harlot the debauchery, affluence and secularism of Rome. If John were writing today, how might he describe 20th century civilization and culture?

DESTRUCTION OF BABYLON

1. Read Rev. 18:1-8. What is the cause of Babylon's downfall (v. 3)?

2. What is the call to God's people (v. 4)?

3. Early Christians may have been tempted to compromise with Babylon in order to escape persecution. If they chose to identify with the worldly Babylon, what then could they expect (v..4)?

4. What characterized Babylon's sins (vv. 5-8)?

5. How is God's punishment of Babylon described (vv. 5-8)?

6. Read I John 2:15-17. Here is really the same call as in Rev. 18:4— a warning to keep from becoming identified with the godless world system. For you personally, what is the most subtle temptation from the world?

THE LAMENTS OF BABYLON'S FOLLOWERS

1. Read Rev. 18:9, 10. Name the first group to lament Babylon's destruction.
   a. What has been their relationship to Babylon?
   b. Why do they weep and wail? What has the city meant to them?
   c. Do they recognize that judgment has come upon Babylon (v. 10b)?

2. Read Rev. 18:11-17. What group now takes up the lament?
   a. Why does this group weep and mourn?
   b. Note the cargoes that came to affluent Rome, including slaves, human souls (v. 13b). In what ways does modern "Babylon" traffic in human souls?
   c. What had the city meant to the merchants (vv. 15, 16)?

3. Read Rev. 18:17b-19. Name the third group which wails over the city.

a. Why do they mourn?

b. How is the suddenness of the city's devastation described (vv. 10b, 17, 19b)?

THE CALL TO REJOICE

Read Rev. 18:20. Who are called on to rejoice? Why are they to rejoice?

This is not a petty, vindictive cry, but a glad, triumphant shout of joy because every wrong that Christians have suffered will some day be set right and righteousness will triumph over sin.

THE FINAL LAMENT OVER BABYLON

1. Read Rev. 18:21-24. How is the final overthrow of Babylon symbolized?

2. What things will be found "no more" in the city?
State them in contemporary expressions.

3. What is the reason for the destruction of the city (vv. 23b, 24)?

SOME APPLICATIONS

1. Why do you think that the godless world system is pictured as both a harlot and as a city?

2. Is it possible for the Christian to co-exist with the "world"?
If so, what would characterize the situation?

3. What encouragement would these chapters have for persecuted Christians of any age, who have had to forfeit their jobs and lose their possessions because of their faithfulness to Christ?

4. Do you think that the energy and economic woes which are besetting the world today may be a blessing in disguise, especially for us in the United States? Think in terms of these chapters.

5. What prayer concerns do these chapters bring to mind? Write them down and pray about them.

LESSON X

CHRIST IS KING OF KINGS AND LORD OF LORDS

REVELATION 19 & 20

INTRODUCTION TO THE STUDY

1. Think through the Revelation and review the songs in the book. Find one song in each of the following chapters: 4, 5, 7, 11, 14, 15, 19. Record your findings under the following headings: *Chapter reference, Who Sings, To whom, Theme of song.* Use another sheet of paper.

2. Glance at the chart (p. 5) and note that the three series of judgments are over and that God's great "mop-up" has begun.

What was the first enemy to be eliminated (Rev. 17, 18)?

3. Read Rev. 19, 20. What enemies are eliminated in these chapters?

4. How many contrasts can you find between the last lesson (Rev. 17, 18) and Rev. 19? Think in terms of the two women, the groups, the songs and the mood.

THE HALLELUJAH CHORUS

(Read Rev. 19:1-8)

1. How many hallelujahs are sung by the heavenly choirs?
    a. Who sings the first two hallelujahs?
    b. What is the reason for this outburst of song (v. 2)?

2. Who join in the triumph song on the third hallelujah (v. 4)?
What does their "Amen" indicate?

3. Who are next invited to join this universal song of praise (v. 5)?

4. Who sings the fourth hallelujah (v. 6)?
    a. How would you describe this music (note "like the sound of . . .")?
    b. What two reasons are given for this song of praise (vv. 6-8)? (Each reason is preceded by *for*, RSV).

5. Wherein is this hallelujah chorus really a climax to all the songs in the Revelation?

THE MARRIAGE SUPPER OF THE LAMB

(Read Rev. 19:7-10)

1. What is meant by *the marriage supper of the Lamb?*
Who is the bride?   the Bridegroom?   Who are invited?

2. Contrast the clothing of the bride (v. 8) with that of the harlot (Rev. 17:4 and 18:16). What does this contrast point up?

THE TRIUMPH OF THE KING OF KINGS

(Read Rev. 19:11-16)

1. As we read these verses there is no doubt as to the identity of this rider on a white horse. It is our triumphant Lord Jesus! List all the things stated about Christ in the symbolic description. Try to state it in your own words. Where have you read some of these descriptions before?

2. Who accompanies Christ when he comes again?

Some have interpreted the robe dipped in blood as referring to judgment — the blood of Christ's enemies. It may also refer to the blood of the atonement. If so, why is it significant that Jesus' robe is sprinkled with blood and his armies' robes are pure white?

3. How would this vision of the conquering Christ bring encouragement to afflicted believers?

THE DEFEAT OF THE BEAST AND THE FALSE PROPHET
(Read Rev. 19:17-21)

1. Contrast the supper of the lost (Rev. 19:17, 18) with the marriage supper of the Lamb.

2. Note the groups which will be at this supper (v. 18). Compare this with Rev. 6:15. What do you note?

3. What forces gather to make war against Christ (v. 19)?
   a. What is the outcome of the conflict (vv. 20-21)?
   b. What weapon does Christ use to defeat the enemy (Rev. 19:15)?

4. Every person will take part in one of the two suppers mentioned in this chapter. Which one it will be will depend on one's response to Jesus' invitation in Rev. 3:20. Why is this so?

EVERY ENEMY DEFEATED
(Read Rev. 20)

Chapter 20 is another of the very difficult chapters in the Revelation. We must approach it with humility and love and a willingness to listen and learn.

1. Read Rev. 20:1-3. Note the names given the dragon.
Where was he bound?   Why?

What may this binding of Satan symbolize?
(It is well to remember that throughout Revelation, Satan never has a free hand. He is always controlled and restrained by God.)

2. What do you learn about the state of the martyrs from John's vision (Rev. 20:4-6)?

What would this vision of the martyrs mean to persecuted first-century Christians?

3. Read pp. 77-80. What are some possible interpretations of the first resurrection (Rev. 20:5) and of the 1000 years?

4. Read Rev. 20:7-10. When will Satan be loosed?
   a. What will he do when he is set free (vv. 8, 9)?
      (It seems God will use him to bring on the End. God is in control.)
   b. How is the *vastness* of the hosts of the wicked who oppose God in the final battle symbolized?
   c. Against whom do they direct their attack?
      If the city Babylon symbolizes man opposed to God, what may the "beloved city" symbolize?
   d. What happens to Satan?
      Who else is with him?

THE FINAL JUDGMENT

(Read Rev. 20:11-15)

1. Try to visualize the solemnity of this scene. To what are your eyes drawn first?

2. Who will stand before the great white throne (vv. 12, 13)?

3. On what basis will the dead be judged?
   Is this a contradiction to salvation by faith alone (see James 2:26)?

4. Name all the enemies that are now out of the way. (Include the three in vv. 14, 15).

5. What is the meaning of *the book of life?*
   How can you be sure that your name is in the book of life? (See 1 John 5:12; John 5:24.)
   Are you sure that your name is there?

SING HALLELUJAH!

Someone has called the Hallelujah Chorus of Rev. 19 "the wedding march of the Church." What do you think is meant by this?

Listen to a recording of the Hallelujah Chorus from Handel's *Messiah*. As you do so, praise God for that day when all sin and evil will be no more and Christ will indeed be King of Kings, and Lord of Lords!

LESSON XI

NEW PEOPLE IN A NEW WORLD

REVELATION 21:1 - 22:5

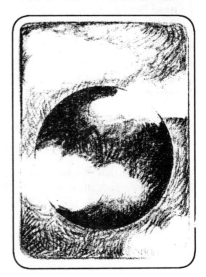

INTRODUCTION TO THE STUDY

• We should really begin this study with a joyous "Hallelujah!" for now the struggles, sufferings and judgments are over. Every enemy has been defeated, Christ is King of kings and Lord of lords. We are about to view the celestial city and learn something about life in the new heaven and earth.

1. Think through the book of Revelation and try to visualize the movement of the book by recalling the name of each chapter or a key idea from each chapter. Try to recall also the larger divisions of the book. Can you do this without referring to the chart?

2. Read Rev. 21-22:5; then scan Genesis 1-3. What contrasts do you find between the first and last chapters of the Bible? Any fulfillments? Record your findings under these headings:

First Creation   *New Creation*

THE NEW HEAVEN AND THE NEW EARTH
(Read Rev. 21:1-8)

1. What does John see (vv. 1, 2)?

a. What has happened to the first heaven and earth (v. 1)? See also 2 Peter 3:10-13. What means will God use to restore, purify and renovate this world?

b. The new Jerusalem seems to symbolize two things. What are they (Rev. 21:2, 9, 10)?

The fact that the new Jerusalem comes down from heaven seems to indicate that there will be "heaven on earth"—God's Utopia—in which God's people will dwell.

c. The meaning of the marriage supper of the Lamb is given in Rev. 21:3. What will be the crowning joy of that event?

2. What seven evils will be "no more" in the new city (Rev. 21:1, 4; 22:3, 5)? (For the symbolic meaning of the sea, (v. 1) see Isa. 57:20 and Rev. 13:1).

a. Why would the elimination of these evils have special meaning for first century Christians?

b. As you contemplate a perfect world, what would you add to the list of things to be eliminated which would have meaning for our world today?

3. Who is speaking (v. 5)? What assurance does he give that what he has promised will come to pass (vv. 5, 6)?

4. What do the words, "all things new" mean to you? What do you want made new?

What is the meaning of his promise in v. 6 and v. 7?

5. Why does John interject the warning in v. 8 and v. 27?
(Remember, John is writing in time, even though he is describing things beyond time.)

THE BEAUTIFUL NEW CITY (Read Rev. 21:9-22:5)

1. Note the prominence of the Lamb in the new Jerusalem. Can you find seven references to the Lamb? What does this emphasis indicate?

2. The new Jerusalem, which symbolizes the kingdom of God on earth, is described in terms familiar to John's contemporaries, a city with walls and gates (Rev. 21:12-14). What would the symbolism of walls and gates suggest to first century Christians concerning this new city?

3. What is John's first impression of the city as he sees it descending from heaven (Rev. 21:2, 11)?

4. Whose names are on the gates of the city (Rev. 21:12)?
Whose on the foundations (Rev. 21:14)?
What is the symbolic meaning of these names?

5. How is the great size of the city portrayed (vv. 15-17)?
The city is a perfect cube, as was the Holy of Holies of the Old Testament tabernacle. What may this symbolism suggest?

6. How is the beauty of the city symbolized (vv. 18-21)?

7. Why is there no need for a temple or created lights in the city (vv. 22, 23)? What does this tell us about the city?

8. How does John portray the *universality*, the *safety* and *openness* of the city (vv. 24-26)?

9. What will guarantee one's residence in the city (Rev. 21:27b)?

How may we be sure that our names are in the Lamb's book of life (see I John 5:11-13; I John 1:9)?

LIFE IN THE CELESTIAL CITY (Read Rev. 22:1-5)
1. In the center of the city is pictured a lovely garden through which flows a river. Note these facts about the river (Rev. 22:1):

    a. What does the river contain?

    What is its appearance?

    What is the river's source?

    b. What do these symbolic descriptions tell us about eternal life in the celestial city?

2. Recall what is said about the tree of life in the garden of Eden (Gen. 3:24).

What change has taken place in the garden (Rev. 22:2)?

What has caused this change?

3. Life in the new heaven and earth will not be monotonous or boring but filled with meaningful service. What will it be (Rev. 22:3b)?

4. Read I John 3:2. Then read Rev. 22:4. Close your eyes and meditate on these words, "I shall see his face!" What do these words mean to you?

FOR MEDITATION AND PRAYER
Many Christians feel that the greatest experience awaiting them is to go to heaven to live in joyous fellowship with Christ and one another in a perfect new world. As you contemplate the beauty and joy of being new people in a new world, what do you anticipate? Write a few short prayers of praise and thanksgiving expressing your hopes.

As you pray the petition in the Lord's Prayer, "Thy kingdom come," remember these chapters describe that for which you are praying.

LESSON XII

HE IS COMING SOON

REVELATION 22:6-21

INTRODUCTION TO THE STUDY

1. The book of Revelation focuses on Christ and his coming. Think through the book and answer these questions: What picture of Christ do you get from this book? How is he presented? What are the many names by which he is called? What are his activities? Has this study made a difference in your view of Christ? If so, how?

2. The book of Revelation presents a striking contrast between those who follow the Lamb (Christians) and those who follow the beast (non-Christians). Try to recall the contrasts between these two groups, in terms of the object of their worship, their goals, their ultimate end and whatever other contrasts you can see.

Followers of the Lamb   *Followers of the Beast*

THE AUTHENTICITY OF THE MESSAGE OF THE REVELATION

1. John states in Rev. 22:6, "These words are trustworthy and true." Read Rev. 22:6-21 to find assurances that the message of the book is reliable and true. Note especially v. 6b, v.8 v.16.

2. Has the study of the Revelation and these assurances of its reliability changed your outlook on this book? How?

THE IMPORTANCE OF THE MESSAGE OF THE REVELATION

3. What instruction is given to John (v. 10?)

   a. Why do you think it is important that this book be opened to people for study?

   b. What warning and encouragement does v. 11 hold?

4. What warning is given in vv. 18 and 19?

   a. What things in this book might a person be tempted to take away?

   Why would it be such a serious offense to take them away?

   b. What might a person try to add?

THE CLAIMS OF CHRIST

5. In each of these verses note *who is speaking* and the *claim made:*

   | Who Speaks | Claim—"I am . . ." |

   Rev. 22:12, 13

   21:5, 6

   1:8

   1:17

   a. How do these verses show that Jesus claims to be true God?

   b. Why is it important to believe that Jesus is true God?

6. Note the terms Jesus uses to describe himself in Rev. 22:16b.

a. What claim is he making by his reference to David?

b. The morning star heralded the rising of the sun and the breaking of a new day. What is Jesus affirming when he refers to himself as the *morning star?*

THE SEVEN BEATITUDES IN THE REVELATION
7. In each of the following references note what conditions must be fulfilled in order that we may have the blessing.

Rev. 1:3
14:13
16:15
19:9
20:6
22:7b
22:14

a. The sixth beatitude (Rev. 22:7b) promises a blessing to those who *keep* the words of this book. *To keep* involves the total personality, mind, emotion, will. How has the study of this book influenced or blessed you in each of these areas?

What has the study motivated you to *do?*

b. The seventh beatitude assures entrance into the celestial city to those who "keep on washing" (Greek tense of verb) their robes. What is meant by the robes and how are they cleansed? (See I John 1:7, 9.)

THE GRACIOUS INVITATION TO COME TO CHRIST
8. What is the condition for coming to Christ (v. 17b)?
a. What are some indications that one is thirsty for the water of life?

b. How does one drink the water of life? (See Rev. 3:20)

c. As a response to Jesus' gracious invitation, say quietly this prayer by Martin Luther:

"Ah, dearest Jesus, Holy Child, make thee a bed, soft, undefiled, within my heart that it may be a quiet chamber kept for thee."

SOME ADVENT THOUGHTS

9. What is John's response to Jesus' promise to come again (Rev. 22:20b)?

a. How do you feel about his coming again? How do you respond?

Do you wish Jesus would hurry his coming, or would you rather that he delay awhile? Why?

b. How will you incorporate your study of Revelation into your life from now on?

PRAISE AND THANKSGIVING

Close your study with prayers of praise and thanksgiving for the blessings which the message of the Revelation has brought to you. Write out your prayers (on another sheet of paper if you wish).

SING JOYFULLY that great song of the faith, "How Firm a Foundation" which expresses the message of the Revelation so meaningfully or sing that joyous hymn "Joy to the World," or listen to some of the glorious music from the Messiah.

POSTSCRIPT

And now may the promised blessings of this book continue to abide with us until faith becomes sight when we will see Christ and one another in the beautiful city of God, forever singing praises to our Lamb.